The Paper Plane Plan

ROSS DAVIES

DEDICATION

For my wife and family.

CONTENTS

ACKNOWLEDGMENTS

Thank you to the full Strafe Creative family for all your help with this book. To my family and friends for putting up with me over the years, and of course my beautiful wife.

1 WELCOME

Thank you for picking up my book to read. Over the years, I've found I'm always looking at ways to improve my business and sales, tweaking things and trying out different experiments. I think this lead me down this route of growth hacking and experimentation. I think this can be traced back to where I started in life and what I've learnt along the way.

Years and years ago, I studied engineering at university and I was really interested in how everything fitted together, along with the intricacies that go into making something. I never really lost that passion even though I now own a design agency. After university I had a couple of different jobs. One was working for a games company, which was interesting to see the inner workings of that industry. It was a 24 hour, consistently accessible game and I was always amazed at how the designers and developers would tweak the game based on how users were playing it. It was amazing to see how this real-time data could affect the game's design.

I initially started in their customer service department. After learning about the players I then moved into the graphics side of things and got involved with 3D modeling. I loved being able to build items for the game from scratch. I was also able to join in with the marketing, which helped to shape what I eventually moved into. Being able to get some a vast experience from one industry is what really helped drive my passion for running all these little experiments. As they were a big games company, they were willing to throw money into ideas to see what really worked. I loved that whole side of it and that's what made me decide to set up Strafe Creative and do this myself.

I really wanted to be able to run with my own ideas and have full control. That's what's exciting to me, coming up with an idea and see tangible results very quickly.

I guess that's what also led to this book. I was always running experiments and people starting asking for advice when they saw them succeed. So, I thought the best option would be to get my ideas down on paper and try to help even more people.

Now the book title mentions Growth Hacking, which is a very on trend term at the moment. But let's first define what Growth Hacking is, well this is how Wikipedia defines it:

A process of rapid experimentation across marketing channels and product development to identify the most effective, efficient ways to grow a business.

To be honest, this is an awesome explanation for it but the problem is that growth hacking is very much focused on the tech industry. That's mainly because tech companies interact with their clients on a computer which means everything is fully trackable. This is great for them, because when they run a test they can quickly look at the stats and know it's a success. But guess what, I don't run a tech company. I run a Design Agency, which for all intent and purpose is in the service industry. So, when I looked into growth hacking for service companies or professional services, there isn't any advice on it.

In an ideal world, growth hacking would mainly be used by SAAS companies. In this book I'll refer quite a lot to SAAS, which stands for: "Software as a service."

The easiest way to explain SAAS is with an example, so let's quickly run through one.

Adobe Photoshop.

Photoshop is a graphic design software. Customers would purchase their Photoshop software for a couple hundred quid and could then use this how they liked. What slowly happened though was customers, instead of purchasing, started to pirate the software (download the software illegally for free).

So what Adobe cleverly did was to change their model so that you had to pay monthly for it. They then gave constant updates which were included in the cost, but meant the user could no longer just download one big version and have everything. This is a super clever idea and actually Windows now do the same with their "office" products. Previously, you purchased copies of Microsoft Office and that was yours to put on your computer, whereas now you have to pay a monthly fee. It's normally a tiny amount but it's a much easier way for them to run their business, by having monthly fees and profits, which is why running SAAS is so popular now.

E-commerce stores are another popular area for Growth Hacking. This is because the entire customer journey is done through either a website or email. This means the entire journey can be tracked, tweaked and tested. That's basically what growth hacking is all about. I guess it's just a buzz term for trying out little experiments, tweaking the intricacies of your website or your different software's, and monitoring what helps to increase the number of people who buy from you. Simple really.

Now if you've picked this book up, you're probably in the service sector. We're not selling a product that's standard, most service companies are providing something bespoke, our customers journeys aren't fully online and we're essentially selling our time.

So that's what this book is all about. It's taking these learnings from tech industries and applying them to service companies.

As I went through the journey of setting up Strafe Creative, I've run all these different experiments and jotting them down. I've learned from them and tweaked them slightly so that they can work really well. This book is the result of this.

I think this all goes back to this fundamental idea that I've always kind of run with:

If you can imagine a Roman temple, it's made up of lots of different pillars going all the way around the edge of it. You can imagine that this building is much stronger and steadier if it's got lots of pillars all the way around it and not just one in each corner. Your business and marketing should work in the same way, with your business being the roof and the marketing all the different pillars. Each pillar should be a different marketing activity. For example a basic standard company may have the following:

- A Website
- Twitter and LinkedIn
- Monthly email
- Networking events

Most people think that's enough. Continuing with my metaphor, that's only one pillar in each corner. That's not going to be very strong and secure to hold your roof up, and therefore not strong enough to hold your business together.

This is where all the different lessons and experiments in this book are going to help. For anyone who is reading this book, I recommend that the simplest and easiest way to work through it is to choose one of the lessons that appeal to you and read it. Finish the rest of the book later. if you love the lesson you've just read, go try it out.

Think about which experiment would be worth trying first and be willing to test them out.

The book isn't meant to be read front to back. Just take the knowledge from it and run with the ideas that work best for your company. If it works, it becomes one of your pillars which makes your business stronger.

The books has also been split into sections. in theory, I'd still recommend reading the entire book, but you'll find the book is split like this:

Planning stage: For people about to start a business, these are the things you should be thinking about. There's still lots of useful information if you already have a business set up, but this is aimed at startups

Mentality: Your mental approach to business is super important, so I've tried to simplify the keys parts down, making it easier for you to grow and scale your business.

Marketing: We're getting into the main parts of the book now. This section is all about marketing that you can be doing to help drive people to either visit your website or get in touch. These are all about growing awareness of your brand.

Web-based: The biggest section of the book. There's lots of great lessons here based on some of the best Growth Hacks I've ever come across. All of these in here are for service companies and are easy for you to implement into your current site to see great results.

Follow up: Most companies don't follow-up. When they do it's unprocessed and doesn't work well. These are follow up techniques and hacks which you can use to increase your sales and conversion rate from proposal to client.

Advanced: Next are some of the more complex or time-consuming growth hacks we've used over the years.

Random thoughts: A number of the lessons in here are based on my love of dissecting other companies' marketing. They don't fit into another chapter, but each one is based on an important lesson learnt from some of the largest companies across the world.

That's it guys, those are the breakdowns!

Now note that not every single experiment will work for your industry. If you're struggling to come up with how a particular lesson relates to your industry or service, drop me a line through the below social media platforms.

Enjoy yourself and hopefully some of these lessons will really stand out to you.

Twitter: ross_davies
Instagram: rossalexdavies or 'strafecreative' for my company.

Good luck!!

PLANNING STAGE

2 YOUR PERFECT CLIENT

So hopefully by now you're starting to realise that service industry growth hacking is slightly differently to the norm and it's great that you want to get involved. The great news is you only need to smash one of the lessons in this book to transform your company!

The starting point is to focus on your perfect client.

Now, lots of people talk about the persona of who they want to attract, but they make the mistake of keeping the spec too broad. This lesson is going to hopefully help you really drill down to your perfect client.

I try to draw a little doodle of my perfect client in the middle of the page and then I start to write out who they are. Are they in a very certain market?

For example, am I just selling to solicitors? As soon as I can label it to just one person, it's a lot easier to sell to.

Another example might be that I only sell to property investors. As soon as we know this, we can start to niche down the criteria even more. So let's say:

- They've got to be East Midlands based (UK).
- They need to own a certain number of properties for you to work with them.
- Over a certain age.
- Willing to invest X amount per year.

As you can see, it's now a lot easier to sell to this person.

That particular system might work well for an accountant. It will be much easier for them to market if they know they're only after high net worth property investors who own more than 20 houses in the East Midlands.

You need to take all of these into account. You need to consider the company's location, their turnover, what they sell and my favorite one, the one I feel is personally overlooked a lot, the person's role in that company.

For example, my company, Strafe Creative, targets Marketing Managers and Managing Directors, depending on the size of the business. As these are the two people I'm going to sell to, there's no reason for me to try to sell to the Head of Finance, as they won't want my offering.

So that's it guys. Before you read any further, we need to drill down into this so you know who you want to work with. The way I also like to do this is imagining only the perfect client. Don't worry if none of your current clients fit the bill, focus on who you want to work with. It's also useful if you already have a company you could aim at.

Exercise

Who is your perfect client? Answer the following:

- Location
- Industry
- Is there a sub industry too?

- Size of business (turnover)
- Number of staff
- Who in the business would you sell to?
- What software do they use?
- What pain points do they have?
- Why would they want to work with you?

To help you, my company, Strafe Creative would be:

- East Midlands UK
- E-commerce
- Selling items over £150 each
- £2m+
- 30+
- Marketing director and E-commerce director
- Magento or Shopify
- Low conversion rate or High advertising costs
- We can increase their conversion rates quickly

It's a great one to start with for any size business, start up or large company. It's always good to take a step back and evaluate this. The reason this is the first lesson is that it sets the foundation for all the other lessons. It also means we're not wasting money or time on the wrong types of clients.

3 NAMING YOUR COMPANY

One of the first things that I've already touched on in Lesson 1 was knowing who your exact target market and perfect client are.

Your name and what it represents is going to be super important. Note that this Growth Hack is probably going to work best for a startup, as I totally understand that to change your name is a big step just to drive up sales. But do have a read of this chapter as it might make you realise that the name you've chosen for your business doesn't really represent what your company is all about. Remember that the name is the first thing a client is going to see about your business. It's their first impression so it's important you get this right!

Let's get into an example to help explain this in more detail. The example we're going to use is a personal trainer company. A personal trainer is a great example of a service industry as, like lots of us, they're selling their time.

Let's look at a couple of different names of this potential personal trainer business.

- Rapid workouts
- Exclusive workouts
- Quantum genetic workouts
- Kettle bell workouts

So, all four of those have very different meanings and feelings to them. 'Rapid workouts' gives the impression that they offer quick workouts that are going to be easy; easy to do and easy to follow. Anything associated with speed also connotes that it's cheap too.

'Exclusive workouts' seems far more expensive and would attract a very different market to 'Rapid workouts'. It seems the most luxurious option out of the four shown.

We've then got 'Quantum Genetic workouts' which comes across as the most science-based option. Their potential customer is going to presume that it might be quite nutrition-based, using lots of statistics and body measuring to get the best out of these workouts.

You can see already that just by changing a word in the name, a potential customer will have a very different feeling towards a business.

We've then got one which is called 'Kettle Bell workouts', which, quite obviously, suggests everything they offer involves using a kettle bell. The problem arises if they introduce more varied equipment in the future; their name would need to change accordingly.

This might not be a major issue for a Personal Training company, but by naming their business after their service, they can't pivot their business as much as they might want to in the future.

As well as the name, we also need to think about how you appear to your customers. Let's now use a real life example, EasyJet.

EasyJet is known for being very cheap and that's why people use them. Whereas Emirates is known as very high-class and expensive. These connotations not only come from their names but also from the way they're portrayed and branded. So if you're going to want to look expensive ensure it's because you're going after high value customers.

Perception is super important so, if you are after high ticket clients, don't choose a name which doesn't represent that.

Exercise:

- Combined with the information from Lesson 1 (Perfect client) start to make a list of potential names which your clients would want in your service.
- List your clients' pain points and come up with names which would fix those.
- List your main benefits and come up with names to get that message across.
- Check Google to see if there is already a company with that name. If so, disregard it and try another.

MENTALITY

4 GOAL SETTING

Before you even think of running your business, or think about re-grouping for the next year, you need to outline what your overall goals are going to be for the year.

Having an end goal makes it a lot easier for you to track your progress. If you have read a Grant Cardone book, you'll know that the whole idea is to go after something that's really big. If your goal is to have a £100k turnover, that's quite easy to achieve. Instead aim for £1 million, so that even if you pull up short, you'll have made more money than if you had aimed for £100k.

Go big with whatever your goals are going to be for the year! You also need to ensure that your goals are "Smart".

You probably already know these, but as a reminder they are:

S - specific
M - measurable
A - action-oriented
R - results-oriented
T - time-based

So a normal goal might be:
" I want to make £1 million"

A smart version of this would be:

"I want to make £1 million by April 1st 2018 through selling 25 a month of service X. I'll sell this service by mainly using cold calling."

Please also know that it doesn't need to be money orientated. Although I'm running a business, my goals for my design agency are more around working with clients we love and getting them huge ROI's. I also want to work with big, well-known clients, but that's just important to me.

I also have personal goals, such as wanting to be well known in our industry and being the person that people turn to professionally. Hopefully you guys reading and enjoying this book will push me towards these goals too. (No pressure!)

For most people, if you haven't done this before, the easiest one to start with is money, so let's use that as an example.

A lot of people make the mistake of just making up a number and having that as their goal. This isn't really the point, as the goal has no meaning. Your main aim should be to work out what will make you happy.

Let's say you're making £24k per year at the moment. Your new goal is £50k but why? Will that help you buy the house you want? The car you want? The holidays you want to go on? The other things you want to buy? Make a list of everything you wish you had and then work out the yearly cost attached to that. Then bingo, we have a starting point! Like I said at the start of this chapter, the idea is to reach for the stars, so take your new goal and times it by five. Now that's your big, scary goal!!

Other examples of goals for your business may be:

- To take on a certain number of staff by a certain date.
- To have a new website sorted by then.
- To have a certain number of monthly retainers in place.
- To have a certain number of speaking that gigs by a certain time.

These are all goals you should be thinking about and having them written down will make a huge difference. Time for some honestly now. My goals for the end of this year were to:

- Have my first book published (you're reading it!)
- Speak at an event with an audience of at least 300 people.

Without these big, scary goals written down, I know I would never have managed them.

Exercise:

- Work through your smart goals and create a list of them. Print out the list and keep them in the following places:
- By your bed to read before bed and when you awake in the morning.
- Inside your bathroom cupboard door to read when brushing your teeth.
- By your work computer, or better yet, as your background on your computer.

5 WOULD YOU BUY FROM YOURSELF?

So let's ask a hard question: would you buy your service? Do you think it's as good as it could be? I am not even sure this is a lesson. It might be more of a rant, but it's a good rant either way, so read on!

In my area there is a local event which has around 150 attendees, as well as a decent sized marketing list. It's run as a not-for-profit and everyone involved is a volunteer. So, although everyone running the business club is a director of his or her own business, it's always a side project for everyone. That's not a knock at all, it's amazing these guys all want to be involved and help their community. But they had some big plans to grow their offerings. The event made all of its money from sponsorships each year and each year it struggled to get these in. Because of their aggressive growth plans they needed to raise double in sponsorships to the year before.

Now I love these events. They serve great food, give out free drinks, and its relaxed yet professional.

Unfortunately, they couldn't hit their new target. It's always a bit of struggle but it was even harder because of the higher target. People just weren't biting and after four months they we're running out of options.

In the background I had wanted to get more involved and help out, so I joined the group which ran the event.

We ran through the issues and they spoke about what a great opportunity it was and that they couldn't understand why people hadn't signed up. Which by accident lead me to ask "As you help run the event, are you guys not allowed to also sponsor it? Is it seen as a conflict of interest?".

I was then hit with some stuttering, followed by excuses such as:

- It's very expensive
- We don't have that sort of money to spend
- It's not our target market
- We've already accounted for our marketing spend for the year.
- Which, when you read between the lines, essentially means:
- "I don't see the value in this".

They were 100% correct. Their offering was weak, not attractive, and in no way good value for money.

Now to me the answer should be obvious. I want the offering to be so awesome and so useful to me that even if I'm running it, I want to sponsor it too. We want people to know exactly what they'll be getting for their money and realise what an opportunity it is! Surely that's what we all want for our own companies?

As you know, I run Strafe Creative and I 100%, believe in our work. I know for a fact that whether you spend £20k, £50k or even £100k with us, it's going to pay for itself within 3 - 6 months because of the expertise we have and the track record of our projects. We all love the work we do and in a heartbeat believe that great design can truly transform a business.

No one is going to buy your service if you don't believe in that offering. If you can imagine a car salesmen working for BMW, I feel like they should own a BMW. Not the cheaper option either. I believe they should be driving around in the top spec version. The cars with bigger engines, better looks, the cars people really want to own. If the salesmen aren't willing to shell out for one of those, and they work for BMW, then why the hell should I listen to a word they say?

If they're too stingy and don't see the value in owning the BMW, then how can they possibly inspire me to instead?

Exercise:

So it's time to ask yourself the question, would you purchase your own service at the price you charge? If so great! How could you add even more value?

If you wouldn't, why is that? What could you add to your offering to make you want to buy it? Once you start to believe in your own service you'll have a much easier time selling it to others.

6 WHY DESIGN IS SO IMPORTANT

Warning, warning! Understandably I believe heavily in the power of design but hear me out. To me design matters, always has, always will.

I believe design is the number one way you will attract your perfect client. Now this can only be done with the use of the other chapters, but as a quick recap: You now know who you want to work with. You need to know every tiny thing about them, as it will affect how you portray your business and your brand's:

- Colour choices
- Marketing material
- Website
- Tone of voice in text
- Price point

Let's start with a cheap brand:

This is for the people with a cheap service, for the people working with a 'sell it cheap and stack them high' approach. You just want to get it out to the mass market. You want everyone to buy it and you know it's cheap. The best example I can think of is EasyJet.

EasyJet are a budget airline travel company. They are super cheap and proud of it. Everything about them looks and feels cheap, it's all part of their brand. Orange in design is very much seen as a value colour, so it's no surprise that they've chosen this as their brand colour.

Their websites are basic and functional. They don't want them to look fancy and premium as nothing else they do is. They're purposely making themselves looks cheap because that's their market. They know what they offer and that's cheap flights.

On the opposite end of the spectrum are the premium colours, such as dark blue and regal purple. For example, Cadbury Dairy Milk was originally in purple because the colour purple was so expensive to print. They wanted the brand to be premium and expensive. So without any indication of price, you could have looked at the wrapper, back when it was first launched, and know it was expensive.

Ok sweeping statement time! That is "You get what you pay for". If you spend £5K on a car you know it's probably very old or very cheap. It won't be very fast, the build quality is likely to be low, but it will do the job.

Spend £40k on a car and you can get yourself a nice BMW. It'll be quick and it'll come with leather seats that are super comfortable. It'll be nice to drive and will last ages. Now both of the cars do the exact same thing, they take you from point A to point B. But there's a reason most people want the BMW, it's the feeling it gives its owners. There are hundreds of cheaper options, but people line up to purchase the BMW because it's designed to look and feel premium.

This dedication to the details and how you come across should be ingrained into your business. For example, if you're selling an expensive product with is £3000 per item, you can't spend £500 on your website and £500 on your branding, as the quality of the work will be sub-par and will cheapen how you come across.

Let's use another example. We had a client selling bean bags. It was a really decent sized business and had awesome people running it too. So they were the perfect business to get involved with. Their entire business rested on their website. All marketing funneled people to the site and the only way to order a bean bag was through their site.

But they were always having the same issue, people were buying their cheapest options and if they did get calls or messages on live chat, it was always about the quality. They would even get reviews left saying they were surprised at the quality of their products! So there was this big issue with how the public perceived them. Now their bean bags weren't cheap by any means. We're talking £200+ for a bean bag, so, from a price point of view, they we're a top tier seller.

The issue arose by how they appeared. Their brand, website and marketing material all made them look cheap and cheerful. This explained why people only bought their cheapest offerings; they were the only ones they trusted from them. Now this just goes to show the power of design. When the bean bag company started out they did all the design themselves. They didn't know any different.

With their new range of bean bags they were releasing, and the growing number of students and young professionals purchasing bean bags, they knew they had to change.

We did this in small steps with them, to prove our theory. We first changed their colour from bright orange to blue, which made a huge difference to their look and sales. Next we got them to invest in new photography. Personally, great photography is an excellent way to add credibility to any of your marketing. It's so easy to take a photo on your phone now, that companies that do invest in top quality photography stand out and notice the change almost immediately.

Now is the time to take a step back and really make a decision on if you're attracting the right market for you. Setting realistic budgets is also going to be needed. If you're only spending £500 on your design work but charging your service out at £10k, then you're going to have a huge problem selling.
In all likelihood, your current, cheaper appearance is devaluing your main offering. It's as simple as that.

There is a well-known rule called "the 5 second rule". It's the rule that you have made a judgement on someone or something within the first 5 seconds.

Let's discuss some of the worst things that happen.

- You're wearing a badly fitted, cheap-looking suit which cost you £100, but you're a financial advisor (I see this all the time, it's crazy to me!!).
- You meet someone at an event and they hand you their business card. It feels super thin and flimsy because they skimped on paying for quality ones.
- You're a personal trainer but can't afford your own uniform.
- You're an accountant with no letterheads.

All these little touches, including how you appear to your potential clients, can hugely affect them wanting to work with you.

My thought process is if you're not willing to invest in your own business, your own appearance, and how you're portrayed to the public, you're probably not willing to invest in creating a great service either. Unless I'm wanting to spend as little as possible, I'm probably not going to spend anything with you. You must have confidence in your own services to be willing to invest in them, and once you do, you'll see a big spike in sales.

7 EASY MATH

I'm not going to lie, this idea is taken from the sales master known as Grant Cardone. It's tweaked to apply better to you guys and I use it heavily, not just for sales, in multiple parts of my life.

Easy math is all about breaking down your figures into really digestible mouthfuls (I love a good food reference). Let's say you're just starting out and you think even making £50k is going to be hard. But if you break that down into small chunks actually this becomes very manageable to achieve.

Let's do an example where we're aiming to make £1 million. Let's look at the different ways you could do this:

1. You could get 5000 people to buy a £200 service from you. Then you have £1 million!
2. You could you get 2000 people to buy a £500 service from you.
3. You could get 1000 people to purchase a £1000 service.

Or you might be aiming to have clients on monthly retainers. If that's the case:

4. 5,000 people pay you a £17 a month. That gets you £1 million.
5. You're going to have 2,000 people paying you £42 month.

6. 1000 people giving you £83 a month over a year would give you £1 million.

I would imagine that for service companies we're working with much bigger retainers. So let's do just a few more:

7. 167 people paying you £500 a month
8. 84 people paying you £1000 a month
9. 42 people paying you £2000 a month

Hopefully you'll agree that when you're start to break down these figures they become a lot more realistic.

The clever thing with this math is that you will have multiple ways to get to £1 million. You might have a combination of retainer and main services, along with different services on different retainers. You'll see that when these compound together, it all becomes far more feasible.

Personally, once I know the numbers, it makes it much easier to achieve. Trying to make £1 million seems very daunting if I have no idea how to get there. But if my aim for the year is to sell 42 companies onto a £2k retainer, all of a sudden that doesn't seem too bad!

Exercise:

- Decide on your money target for the year
- Break down your services into one-off costs and retainers
- Work out your average cost (I'm aware most service companies have bespoke costs, but you should know a rough estimate for this)
- Then use your average on your one-off costs to find out how many of these services you need to sell to hit your target
- Do the same with your retainers
- Break these down into monthly sales targets, eg: I need to sell five of these per month
- Get selling!!

8 HOW MUCH ARE YOU WILLING TO SPEND?

That seems like an obvious question, but you may not know the answer. I bet if you asked business owners, most wouldn't know the answer to this question. If they did, the number would be too low.

Let's use one of the daddies of the tech industry for this example, Dropbox!

They didn't necessarily pay people, but they gave away their service for free, which obviously still has a monetary value. When they first set up, every person that referred them got 2GB of storage for free. Also, the person who was referred in got 2GB free too. On top of that you could invite up to ten people which meant users who managed to get 10 of their friends to join got 20GB free. This cost them a fortune to give away!

This growth hack which Dropbox performed is one of the greatest growth hacks I've ever seen. It was a huge win for everyone involved. The company got more customers, the user got free space, and the referred user got free space too. As we all know, 2GB doesn't actually go that far, but once you're already using a system you end up sticking with it and Dropbox knew this.

The reason this worked so well is Dropbox knew other companies wouldn't be willing to front the bill. They knew that the more people on a free account the more people that would eventually become paying customers. As the referral system was a win for everyone involved, they didn't need to spend big on other marketing. Now this is the lesson to learn here: Dropbox was willing to spend because they knew their numbers. They knew how many free accounts they had to get in to convert to one paying customer. As long as that one paying customer covered the cost of the free people, they were on to a complete winner!

Most companies, especially in the service sector, are not willing to spend money to bring in new customers. If they are, they vastly underestimate the cost. We asked over 100 local businesses about this and most answered with either:

1. We run our business based on referrals so don't pay anything (which is a stupid way to run a business!)
2. They having marketing budgets but expect to pay less than £50 a customer

I'm telling you now, if you're in the service industry and charging big costs, £50 is just not enough as a cost per sale.

Let's say I'm selling a service at £5k. In theory, I could spend £4k on getting new clients and I'd still make a profit. Now I know realistically that I've got to pay the staff wages, I've got the pay for the office, rent, electricity and everything on top of this. But to get the point across, let's ignore that for a second.

If to make £5k you have to spend £4k, would you do it? Yes of course you would, as you'll always be making money!

Now let's take this a step further. As mentioned just before, we asked over 100 companies what they spend on client acquisition and most said less than £50. So let's imagine if your company was willing to spend £1000 on client acquisition. All of a sudden we're going to be different to 99% of all the other service businesses.

For example, if you're looking for an SEO firm and you have 2 options:

1. SEO company A- Found them on Google, liked the look of

what they did, and when you spoke to them they booked you in for a meeting to discuss the project in more detail.

2. SEO company B- Found these guys on Google too, same as company A. You again liked what they did but when you rang them, they invited you to an invite-only box at your local arena to watch ice hockey. That way you can get to know the team and they can run through their services in a non-sales environment. After the ice hockey, they booked you in for a sales meeting.

Which one are you going to go with? Easy choice right?

The worst money saving examples are always at trade shows. I love trade shows as a stand tells you a lot about a business. Some companies turn up with nothing but a banner stand and some bits and pieces to hand out. They go with the cheapest space, which is tiny and right at the back of the room. Yes they get some leads, but they have to work damn hard for them and there's only a handful.

Next we have the company that has paid for a bigger area, in a more visible location. Instead of just banners, they've commissioned a full stand with tables and chairs to sit down with potential clients. They've also got loads of free giveaways to attract potential clients over.

Now the obvious question is going to be, who do you think got more leads? Clearly the second one. But what if I told you they bother offered services at £4k each and company A only spent £5k but company B spent £15k.

Now which do you think will be more profitable?

I'm willing to guess that Company B brought in a higher number of quality leads, due to having a more visible, bigger, and professional stand. Not only will they have more leads, but the actual quality of them will be much better.

We all make the mistake of trying to do things on the cheap, but when it comes to clients, really know your numbers and figure out what you really can afford to spend. I promise you that once you start to spend more, the clients will roll in.

9 BANK ROBBERS

Simple question: Why do robbers even rob banks?

They rob banks because that's where the money is. It makes sense to go to an area where there is a large chunk of money in one place. It's better for them to hit one place to get all of their money, instead of going to multiple shops to rob a lot less.

The same applies to everyday life with shopping. Nice, expensive shops congregate and value shops congregate. This is because they know that people will go to those particular locations to get what they need, so it makes sense that all of the relevant shops are together.

Tech companies apply this idea in a really great way. Most tech companies will use some form of accounting software to take payments from customers online. They know there's a ready-made market of people using software such as Woocommerce, Magento, and, Shopify (online shops). So tech companies will purposely build functionality which interacts with this accounting software. Once a tech company has built something useful, they can tell these accounting software companies, such as Magento, about it, who then promote this on their own site. In return, these tech companies essentially gain free marketing. By offering something useful, you have the chance to grab an entire market that want to spend money with you.

From our point of view, as the owners of service-based businesses, we need to need to think of how we can take advantage of this in our market. What is our market spending money on and how can we build or offer something that directly ties into the rest of this market?

This relates back to the start of the book, in which we need to have a decent outline of who we want to work with. A prime example would be if you're an accountant. A lot of accounting software have tests on their websites. These tests allow you to become a registered person in a company's software. You can then advertise your certified expertise, making more people want to use you. But also, people can go on an accounting software's website and, after typing in their postcode, find that you are a local, registered expert in that specific software.

Really quickly you can tie into their market and make yourself known, taking advantage of another company's marketing. HR lawyers do the same thing, partnering with popular HR software so that they can offer it to their clients.

Here at Strafe Creative we also take advantage of this. We do a lot of split testing and there's some really well-known split testing software around, such as Optimizely, HubSpot, and Visual Website Optimizer. We're certified with all of these, meaning we can offer them all on our site, increasingly our credibility. But also, if you try to use their software yourself and are struggling, you can use their site's search facilities to get in touch with us. Based on location, you can find nearby companies that offer that software and learn more about their services.

Another famous example is luxury car companies that have a habit of sponsoring golf clubs. They know, in theory, that the type of person that plays golf may have enough money to afford luxury cars. Perhaps they're semi-retired and looking to spend their money in a different way. Luxury companies will usually advertise that golf clubs can fit in the boot of their cars, because, again, they know that many golfers could potentially afford luxury cars.

Whether it's luxury cars, software or tech companies, look for where your market is already spending money and attach yourself to it, making yourself more money in the process.

10 BECOME ACCOUNTABLE

This next lesson is less related to the software and service industry and more about something we do at Strafe Creative. It's about making yourself accountable and making your goals visible.

For example, you might want to start going to the gym and get in shape. However, it's an effort to go, you're not sure what you'll do there, and have nothing to aim for. The best thing to do is to get yourself a gym buddy, not just for workouts, but because they hold you accountable. You don't want to let them down so you make the extra effort to attend more and they do the same. You don't want to let the side down!

If we take this analogy and apply it to business, you can see how this will be useful. I have a quarterly mastermind that I go to, in which I discuss my plans for the upcoming quarter. We set goals and targets that we aim to hit. This works well because it gives me really clear goals and targets, as well as a path to follow. It also works well because it makes me accountable. I'm quite competitive and want to deliver at my next mastermind. I usually leave these sessions feeling very driven and if there are any lulls I can contact other people from the mastermind to check in and catch up. This is really helpful around deadlines, when I just need that final push to get everything across the finish line.

I have a few other friends who run businesses too, who make their goals visible by posting them on social media. I think letting everyone know helps push yourself forward. The pessimists may say this is a bad thing to do because if you fail, more people know about it. I think this is a positive and the exact reason you should do this. You don't want to let people down and you don't want to be seen as a quitter. It makes you put in that extra 10% which could be the difference in having a successful business

Give this challenge a go guys. We've discussed goal setting in other chapters, now why not make them public? Get it on twitter and tag me @ross_davies.

MARKETING

11 VALUE PROPOSITION –
GIVING AWAY VALUE

Giving things away to build an audience is a standard part of both the software industry and Growth Hacking. But if you're reading this, you're here because you're a service company and that means it's not so easy for us to give things away, as we wouldn't want to give our service away for free.

Let's run with an example of an accounting software. They might give away a 30 day free trial, which is a great idea as it hooks the user into using their service. As it's just software, it doesn't cost them anything to do this.

Now what's really important with us is that if we're going to give something away, it needs to first be of value. It needs to warrant the person to bother. Secondly, it needs to qualify the person as a strong potential lead. Thirdly, it needs to prove you know what you're doing and show how credible you are.

Now this is really hard to do in the service industry, as we're all essentially just selling our time. Time is precious so we don't really want to have to give it away.

At my company, Strafe Creative, a lot of what we do is based on conversion optimisation. We're constantly looking at how people's sites look and work, what kind of people are converting, how many people go into that site and buy, and how we can improve that.

We found that we could add value to our potential clients and help qualify them as a potential leads by screencasting their website. Screencasting is software that records what's happening on the screen as I'm talking. It also records my voice. All we do is look at people's websites and we run through five things that we think they could easily change to increase their number of leads. At the end of the video we mention that we know the prospect will be in a certain number of camps. We know:

- You either like the changes and will just use your current developer.
- You can get us to make the changes and boom we have a new customer.
- You didn't understand how it helps or you didn't watch the video.

Now yes, this takes time to do. It takes us about 30 mins to do each video, but the hit rate of video-to-customer is huge!

In the service industry, we don't need 1000's of leads like a software company. We just need to ensure that we convert the leads we get. This video idea would work really well for lawyers or accountants. The person could send over their current contracts or basic accounts and you could give your thoughts on how these could be improved. It showcases that they are really interested and highlights that you are different to the rest. It's a winner for everyone involved.

What's also great about this is that once they've watched the video, when they get back in touch, they're already sold on working with you. There's no need for the hard sell and you're not wasting time doing lots of meetings. You can instead just sit in your office, record videos, and only meet with the people who seem keen.

We've got a client that is a HR Lawyer and they've designed this awesome diary especially for a HR personnel. If they need advice for certain things, it's all in this diary with loads of explanation sheets.

The diary is perfect for their clients and many can't wait to get hold of a free copy. Whilst it costs to create this free diary, they gain a large database of people who need their service, so it's a total win for everyone.

This is going to be time-consuming for you to do, so you're either going to have to have a large amount of time upfront to create something or spend a little bit of time each day giving something personal away. This is by far the easiest way to generate high-quality leads for a reduced amount of cost. Instead of having to spend thousands on pay-per-click advertising with a conversion rate of one percent, you can focus on high value customers who are using your free, value-added products. When a business is willing to be different, growth happens rapidly and that's what we need to be looking at!

Exercise:

- How could you provide value to potential clients without spending all of your time doing free work?
- Could you start to use video as part of your upfront marketing before meeting clients?
- What tool could you create to give away for free to help identify potential clients?

12 PERSONAL VIDEO

Let's get into video and how to be more personal with it. I think one of the main habits business-to-business companies have is making everything generic, so that they can scale quickly and keep costs down. As we're in the service industry, we don't need thousands of leads, we just need to ensure the ones that come in are of good quality.

I'm going to run through two business coach examples who have both tried to sell to me in the past. Both people run events and this is the main way of attracting people to their business. They get people to the events for a low cost (or sometimes free) and then sell to the room by demonstrating their expertise.

Now one of these business coaches sent out lots of emails to me as I was on their mailing list. They tried to sell to me using generic content. This is easy for them to do and they can hit a lot of people with it quickly. The number of leads it brings in will be low, but for the effort it's ok. After the first two emails, I stopped reading them and just deleted them.

The second business coach sent me only two emails. Both were super short, clearly personalised, and directed me to a video link.

The video was just of him talking to the camera, speaking about me and where we first met. He'd looked up what I was up to at the moment and pulled out the benefits of his upcoming event which were most relevant to me. The video was only about 40 seconds in length and it was absolutely awesome! I signed straight up for the event as I'd never seen anything like it. It was so personalised to just me that there was no way I wasn't going to attend his event. I even took it a step further and rang him and asked him about the videos. He explained it was something he had just started running with and tried to spend a maximum of four minutes on each one, including research. That's when I realised it doesn't take much to personalise a video. He just needed my name, to remember where we met, and a quick look at my Facebook to get me hooked. It was super clever and hopefully you can see how this might apply to you as well.

Now creating these videos is essentially free. The main issue is that it's time consuming. But that's what's so great about it; most can't be bothered to do this, so when you do, you automatically look different to the rest of the crowd!

So once I'd seen the power of video, we started doing them in our own business and below is the process we currently use:

(For context, we review companies websites and tell them how they could improve sales and then send it to their marketing directors.)

I have a quick look at their website, write a very quick script consisting of just bullet points, and then record the videos, lasting no longer than four minutes. I try to spend no more than 15 mins on each one, though I find that once I'm in the groove, they go much quicker.

For some businesses you don't even need to do or say anything. You can literally say the same thing in every single video but mention their name and company to personalise it. The video looks like it's been made to provide them value rather than just to make you money as part of your sales. It's this personalisation which makes people create a bond with you and that's why its conversion rate is so much higher.

I know this sounds like a lot of work and you're right, it could be. But I bet you can already imagine how much higher the videos will convert for your business. It's so easy to do and there's some software that you can use to help you. If you've already got a Mac, you can just use QuickTime to create the video. I use Screencastify which is great because as soon as I save a video, it uploads it straight to my Google Drive. I can then simply email that Google Doc onto a prospect.

If you want to go even more technical we can then use software such as Wistia, which is mentioned in a later chapter. Wistia is an analytical video tool that gives you an idea of how much of the video people are watching. We use Wistia personally and I know if they bother to watch the video more than twice all the way through, bang we're in!

Don't be afraid to upload everything to YouTube etoo. Even if you only get a small number of views, it's better than nothing. You only need to impress one person to get a big sale which could transform your business.

These public videos are all about providing value and making yourself the expert in your industry. The main hurdle with this one is having the mentality and just doing it.

Exercise:

- Taking it easy to start with, take a current client you know well and see if you can upsell something to them.
- Download screencastify or a similar software and record yourself on your screen, talking about something of value to your client.
- Remember to not just sell to them, as they won't care. Instead provide help, tips, and tricks to make it personal to them. Mention their name a lot and at the end ask if they fancy a catch up. I bet it works!
- Once you start to see how this works for your current clients, you can then look to add this into your current marketing strategy.

13 LOGO PORN

First off, a quick apology for the name of this lesson. It's just the name we've always called it in the office and it's kind of stuck.

The idea is quite simple. It's about putting your clients' logos on your website and stealing their credibility.

For example, we've worked with the NHS, universities, and some big, national firms. We use their logos on our site to build our credibility. The idea is that users will see these logos on our site and other marketing platforms and be impressed.

The great thing is that you don't even always need a case study or any other information. The logo is enough to showcase the type of clients you work with. You'll be surprised at what a huge difference this can make.

You could also create a section on your site called "Recognition" and list all of the awards you've won or been finalists for. This again helps you build credibility as you must be good if you've won some awards!

Don't worry about explaining the awards or how you won them. At the end of the day, the user doesn't really care what the award was for. Just slap the logo on and that's more than enough for you to build credibility.

You could also showcase any certified partners or different software that you have. This can be really useful, especially for tech areas. If you're selling websites or search engine optimisation and are associated with a certain software, have their logos on your site. For example, we're accredited with Optimizely and Visual Website Optimizer, so we have both of these logos on our website. People who know what this software is are more likely to want to work with us, especially if they know that we're certified.

A great way of displaying this logo porn is to just have strip of them to break up your website's design. Alternatively, you can slot them in between blocks of text to help break up the design and make everything look more visual.

It works really well and is really simple to do. It is a key, easy lesson that adds some credibility to your site. We've covered this before but obviously the more credibility your site gives you, the more leads you're going to get from it.

Whilst on the software front, I also want to explain how we approached this idea for an accounting client of ours. They work with companies big and small, so don't have a niche. Their broad approach means they are willing to work with pretty much anyone and with lots of different types of accounting software.

Now accounting software isn't hugely varied and most accountant firms will only really work with the big three (in the UK anyway). But our client was skilled in over 12 different softwares. Having learnt this, we added all of these logos to their website and explained how they had expertise in all of this software.

Nearly over night they saw an increase in their leads. Don't underestimate how powerful this option can be for you.

Exercise:

- Make a list of your top 10 clients (in term of best known. If you don't have this, it's best to go off the size of the business)
- Make a list of the awards you've won
- Make a list of any accreditations you have
- Make a list of any partners you have
- Make a list of any software you offer

Get these added into your marketing. I would recommend not adding them all on, as that would be a logo overload. Instead, test them out and see which ones people respond to best.

14 EMAIL SIGNATURES

In theory, this is a nice easy lesson guys, but please don't underestimate the power of this hack. It's one of my favorites and we use it constantly with epic results!

Now first, let's explain why this works so well. On average, in our office, and I would imagine in most people's office, people are sending between 30 to 50 emails every single day.

Combine this with the fact that most people don't notice or react to a marketing message on first view, they have to see something numerous times before they will respond to it. That's why email signatures are an amazing way to advertise.

If we think of the average email signature, it will include: your name, job title and some contact information. That's it!

Why not flip that and give something of value to every single person that you email?

All of a sudden, a standard way of communicating becomes one of the best and easiest ways to drive sales. I almost don't want to include this in the book and just keep it to myself.

The first thing to note is that we don't want loads of text in a signature. People just won't read it. Instead give a short sentence, a small teaser, which gets the user to want to click the link to learn more. For example, you may be giving away a book, free tickets to an event you're talking at, or you've got something new that you want to show off.

Let's use Strafe Creative's most successful example. We were trialing a new service and wanted people to fill out a short, three-question questionnaire. In return, they would get a 50% discount on our new service. As part of this experiment, the email signature was the only place we advertised this. After two weeks, we had 36 people fill in the questionnaire, with five of those people eventually taking up the new service. I want to really emphasis that this was just from having an email signature which told people that we had a new service and wanted their thoughts on it. No cost was involved and within only two weeks, we had amazing results. The email signature is now our go-to place to advertise new things.

What I love about this hack is that you never know where your new sales will come from. For example, you might be emailing a supplier of yours, trying to sort out an issue, and they then click your link and you have a brand new lead! We've even had people trying to sell to us then instead buy from us!

It's so simple and quick to do and that's why I love this grow hack. Give it a try!

15 REVIEWS

This lesson covers the use of reviews and why they rock. We're going to go back to the basics. For someone to know that you offer a good service, you obviously need to get a testimonial or review from your clients. We want to make it as easy as possible for us to get that information and we want to showcase this in a simple way. For me, these are the main goals.

First off, we want to make sure that your clients rate you on some form of star systems. Five stars are great to use as they're very visual and easy for a potential customer to see. Overall, a star system is much easier to view than having to read a full testimonial.

You then want a testimonial from your client. If you're going to get a testimonial, you don't want it to be too long. You don't really want it any longer than about 100 words, which is just a couple of lines. If it's too long, the potential customer on your website won't read it. We need to make sure it's short and snappy.

A key mistake that people make is not having all of the required information for a testimonial or review. Make sure you've got a full name on there, a job title, and the company that they work for.

One of the most important points to feature is their job title, as potential clients can relate to that job role. By listing the role, it gives the users on your website an indication of the title of people you want to work with. It also puts them at ease that you have worked with their job type previously.

So let's explain in more detail why we need all of these parts in a testimonial, starting with the company name. Even if it's a small, unknown company, having their name included in the testimonial will put people's minds at rest. They can at least look up the company on Google. You'll be surprised at the number of fake testimonials you'll see on websites. It's also worth having an image of the person because even if someone doesn't recognise the name or company, they might remember the person's face.

As soon as someone lands on your website, we want them to be super impressed and for you to appear super credible. Reviews and testimonials allow you to achieve this. It's important to not just put all of your reviews and testimonials onto a review page. This means the user would have to actively choose to visit that part of your site. The likelihood is that if they're bothering to read that, they're already reasonably interested. As the customer journey is slightly different for everyone, your testimonials should be on every other page. They should be dotted through the design so that no matter where they are in the customer journey, they'll see your reviews and testimonials, building up your credibility.

Next, you guys need to know how best to get these testimonials from clients. The standard approach is just to email them. I find we've always gotten a better response when it doesn't feel corporate and instead feels super friendly. Something along the lines of:

"Hey XXXX,
Great working with you on XXXX project. We'd love to add your site to our website portfolio and would like to get a short testimonial from you guys to feature. It only needs to be a sentence or two long and if you could also give us a score out of five that would be great, thanks."

At Strafe Creative, we use a bit of software called reviews.co.uk. It's an automated system which allows you to type in your client's email, their name, and what service you provided for them. It then sends your client an email and asks them to rate it out of five. The magic happens when it collects all those reviews and allows you to put a widget on your website, so that you can have all of these testimonials dotted around if you want.

Another great thing about reviews.co.uk is that you can use Google Web hooks, which will pull the reviews from your website and publish these next to your Google listings. If you can imagine you typed in "Dentists based in Manchester" and one of the listings had 20 reviews of five stars next to it, you're probably going to want to choose that one. By using this software, before prospects even bother to see your website, they already think you're more credible and better than your competitors. In turn, this will increase your number of sales and leads.

Exercise:

- Get asking!
- Write a script to send to clients and do them in batches of 10. Do this because if you use any automated review software, it will put the date next to the review. It would look very unrealistic if you had all your reviews close together. So space them out. We send ours out once a month.
- Once you have the testimonials, grab their picture from LinkedIn and use their image, full name, company name, and testimonial on your website.
- Ensure to have them on most pages of your website and feature on all of your marketing platforms.

16 TESCO VALUE

This chapter is a nice, simple lesson; don't look cheap!

No one wants to buy something that looks rubbish. A great example of this is from Tesco. (Tesco is a UK supermarket). Years ago, Tesco had a 'Tesco Value' range which sold much cheaper items and had much cheaper packaging, which was white with a blue strip with 'Tesco' in large letters. This range was clearly of a lower quality but it also looked cheap, so that no one wanted to buy it. People only bought it for necessity and people didn't really want to buy it unless they really, really had to.

I remember that even as a joke, someone wore a 'Tesco Value Christmas jumper' (not sold by Tesco!) which was simply white with the Tesco Value label on. This shows that no one really wants to buy something that looks cheap and not putting effort into appearance is a really easy way to lose sales. I'm slightly biased as I run a design agency, but this can relate back to your cars, your house, and any of the items in your house. Remember, this is the reason that iPhone and Macs became popular. They're useful but they were also bought because of how they looked and felt.

After a couple of years, they rebranded to 'Tesco Essentials', changing their colour palette and overall design so that it looked more premium. It still wasn't as obviously premium as the other options, but it was of a decent quality and standardised items so that they didn't feel as cheap. The case studies that Tesco released showed that the increase from people buying Tesco Value to Tesco Essentials was through the roof. This was because it was a more accessible product, not just for savers, but for the middle class and those who weren't as conscious about money. These people viewed these products as the Tesco version of a branded product, rather than the value version. Even though they are selling the exact same thing inside, the packaging made a lot more people willing to buy these items. What they had managed to do was remove the stigma attached to their original brand!

You should take your overall appearance into account with everything that you do. If you spent £50 on your logo and £500 on your website, but you're trying to sell to the middle price range of your market, you're going to struggle. Your branding doesn't have to look super premium. In fact, you don't want to come across as something you are not, but there is definitely a balance here.

People are more willing to spend money on something that is perceived as having value. One of the quickest and easiest ways to do that is through your overall appearance and message. If you've not spent much on your branding before, or are already apologising to clients on the state of your website and business cards, you really need to reinvest in something that's going to sell well.

Overall, this is going to make your life easier because every time a client gets in touch with you, you'll be giving off a premium, valuable feeling which builds your credibility. Think about Tesco, google the difference between the Tesco Value and Tesco Essentials design, and you'll notice the difference instantly. As a massive company, it's made a huge impact to them. Now let's make a difference to our own, smaller, service-based companies.

17 LINKEDIN SNOOPING

Now warning here, this is probably going to be the easiest bit of marketing I mention in the book. So in practise this is going to be super simple. Firstly, I'll quickly explain what you need to do, but then I'll spend longer explaining why it's useful and why you should be doing it.

Hopefully, most of you are already using LinkedIn. If you're not, shame on you! Get on it, it's essentially a social network for business professionals and also acts as an online CV. It has some really clever features and one is that it tells you the people who have visited your profile and where they work. The original purpose of this feature was so that you could then contact these people as, in theory, they're looking for someone with your skill set. Or you might have put a proposal out to them and then you can see when they visit your profile, knowing that they're learning about you.

Let's take a step back from this and just break down exactly what marketing is. It's essentially gaining exposure and putting your name and company in front of the right sort of people.

With this being said, one of the simplest ways to do this is to visit the profiles of the people you want to work with on LinkedIn. If they've made a post, maybe comment on it or like it. Depending on how they have their LinkedIn profile, they'll either get a daily or weekly email telling them who has visited their profile and......... tadaa! Your face is featuring in their email and they don't even know who you are!

Now people aren't just going to contact you because they see your face. But what LinkedIn does is inform the user of the following information: Your name, your photo, and your job title.

This is where we can get really clever (or sneaky depending on who you speak to). Most people have a habit of putting down generic job titles like 'Director' or 'Sales Person'. Now, if I see one of those, unless I know the person, I'm probably not going to want to connect with them. But imagine if that job title was bespoke to your needs and wants? I bet they're 100% more likely to at least visit your profile and learn a little more about you.

Let's use my company, Strafe Creative, as an example. My target market is e-commerce managers, so I'm making a conscious effort to visit lots of e-commerce managers profiles, which they'll be informed of. Instead of the generic job title 'Director', I have: 'Helping e-commerce managers increase sales without increasing ad spend'. Which job title is going to encourage them to visit your profile more?

This is where the magic happens. This person has seen your face, name, and new, tailored job title. They decide to snoop at your profile (just like you have done to them) and they may like or not like what they see. But because they've visited your profile, you in turn will now get an email notification informing you that they were curious and have visited you! As simple as that is, you've now gone from totally unknown to them, to on their radar.

This is when we want to strike, when you're in their short-term memory. This is when you try to add them on LinkedIn or even send them a short message. You could even combine this with following them on other social media platforms and you'll be far more likely to have an interaction with them.

Remember that your message shouldn't be sales lead at all to start with. You should either be providing something of value or something potentially non-sales, like inviting them to an event.

That's how to turn a cold lead into a warm, potential lead through the power of stalking! ... Ok maybe we shouldn't call it that.

18 TINY COST

This next lesson is about tiny purchases. Now, SAAS companies are great at making you commit just a tiny, little bit of attention or money to them. You either pay a small fee or use their 'freemium model', which gives you basic access to their software and tools, but with restrictions. This allows you to have a small amount of what they have to offer for a very low price. It's a great way for you to commit to them. This is because from a sales point of view, it's much easier to be sold to once you've already bought from them previously. Now that you know this information, it's really easy to apply this to your main business.

There's a really famous example of a guy who sold really nice, second-hand guitars. He was really clever and bought loads of guitar picks and sold them on eBay for a penny. With the people who bought off him, he'd also send them a flyer with information about his company and a link to his website. Then, because they'd bought from him previously, he also had all of their email details, so he could stay in contact with them. It may seem a big leap from a penny to £500 but because they had already purchased from his company previously, it instantly gave him credibility with them.

It transformed his business because he suddenly had a database of relevant people who had bought from him before, to sell his second-hand guitars to. Overall, it's just a really great way of increasing the number of people who purchase from you.

You can also do this in lots of different industries. If you're in a service company, you could give away a low-cost, short book, in which the price just covers the packaging. A client of ours runs a HR solicitors firm, and they had a diary designed for HR managers. They give it away for £1 on the basis that now someone has bought from them, it will be much easier to sell to them in the future.

So there's lots of little things like this that you can do that work really well. It's important to remember that we want this small purchase to attract your perfect client. For example, just giving away something generic, such as an iPad or a pen, wouldn't be of use. It won't define them as a standout client as, in theory, everyone wants one of those.

You can see how the guitar pick offer was super niche, as it targeted those people who needed that item. So, as well as giving something away for free/low-cost, you need to make sure it's relevant to your clients' needs.

Exercise:

- Write down 5 pain points your clients have.
- Write down 5 'nice-to-haves' that you wish you could offer your clients (that aren't part of your core services).
- Work through the list and look at cheap ways you could fix these 10 points.
- Before spending time on it, ask 15 of your current clients if they would like that solution for £5. (It needs to have a small cost attached so they don't just say yes to be polite). The cash amount doesn't seem to matter. Once you ask someone to pay something they better consider the option.
- If so, you're onto a winner and get the item/mini service produced and offer it to them.
- Then get selling that small, new offering using the other lessons from this book.

19 AWARD ENTRIES

Now common sense would suggest that if you are running a successful, quality business, you should be naturally winning awards for your work and service. People seem to think that most companies get nominated for these and win them off the back of people nominating them for doing a great job. Let's end that myth right now. Companies win awards by entering themselves. They put themselves out there because they think they're good enough and want the exposure and the credibility that comes with winning the awards.

So if I can only give one piece of advice in this chapter, it's that you need to be entering as many awards as possible. At my company, Strafe Creative, we have in-house copywriters and when they're not working on clients' projects, they're entering awards for us. You need to be dedicated as you'll probably only hear back on 25% of the ones you enter. You'll probably only become a finalist for 10% of your entries. Now that's not to put you off, if anything the opposite should be true, that should excite you! You only need to enter 10 a month to become a finalist in one. All of the exposure, credibility, and extra work that you gain from these awards comes from this bit of work.

There is a really good company based in the UK called Boost Marketing. They are an award entry agency which you can pay to enter the awards for you.

Obviously not everyone has the budget for that and I prefer to have control over what's being entered. Instead, they offer a quarterly email which has every single award in your industry for that quarter. You can fill out their sign up form, detailing the industry you're from, and they will send you all the relevant awards that you can apply to.

I would say that as long as you're eligible, enter every award that you can as you never know! You'll find that there are two types of award entries:

1. Simple boxes to fill in with your basic information. There will be lots of entries for these, but I would suggest that you enter these as they're easy to enter.
2. You'll get far more complex ones as well, which could take a few hours to prepare and will ask for financial information on your business as well. If I'm honest, these are normally the better ones to enter because these are the bigger, more well-known awards. Secondly, most people really can't be bothered to enter them, so there will be fewer entries. If you put the time in that it deserves, these submissions can make a huge difference.

Now this next bit is just between us, ok? We entered an award called the Amazon Business awards, which is one of the largest award shows in the UK. I was a finalist for the "Young Entrepreneur of the year". To give you an idea of scale, there were huge companies in attendance and the people in my category were from Waitrose, Sainsbury's, and Tesco. The winner was years younger than me and turning over £3.5 million. Most of the competition in my award category were multi-million pound companies and quite a few of them were household names.

If I'm honest, on the day of the awards I knew there wasn't a chance we were going to win. At the time of the awards, we we're small and only had seven members of staff. Clearly, we were only there because our award submission was so well written!

As it was an Amazon award, we gained loads of exposure and even got on local TV. We met some huge businesses at the event that became clients and we now feature their logos on all of our marketing. This goes back to the point I made before: the big awards are time consuming but most people don't put the effort in, so when you do, you can really stand out.

There are also less obvious benefits to this. Awards can particularly help companies entering tenders. The people on the panel for the tender will view your company as credible because of your awards. They rarely look up more information about you and purely go on the content provided in the tender document. You can imagine that if there are three companies up for a project and you're the only one with five or six awards, before you've even open your mouth, before they've even seen your website or tender document, you're already in the driving seat. You're already more likely to win this project because of the position you've put yourself in.

So, go check out 'Boost Marketing' now! Also, I think it's important to know a few key tricks that we use which makes the whole process much quicker.

As you get into a groove with writing these, you'll find that a lot of them ask similar questions. They even ask for the exact same financial details. So, once you've done two or three, you'll find that the award submissions are pretty similar.

The best approach is to first off spend a full day entering a load of them and then save everything you've done. You can then use these submissions as your scripts to enter other awards every few weeks. They'll need a slight tweak each time but you'll probably only need to spend 40 minutes on one with your saved scripts, rather than three-four hours.

Benefits:

- People want to work with the best in the industry; these awards prove that.
- You'll get free PR by the award holder.
- You'll be able to write about the awards in your own marketing.
- The award shows are always full of quality people, so take your business cards!

- If it comes down to a company with or without awards, the awards will always win.
- As mentioned in the logo porn chapter, you want these on all of your marketing platforms to build credibility.
- You can charge more because you're seen as an authority in your sector.
- People want to be associated with winners.

20 PARTNERSHIP

This chapter is based on a very internationally known concept/company called BNI, which stands for Business Networking International. If I'm honest, I don't particularly agree with their system but follow me with this.

You meet once a week in a room and you're only allowed one person from each industry in there. The idea of a one person's industry is that there's no competition and you pass work between each other. Now the reason I don't particularly like the BNI approach is that if the people in the room aren't particularly good, you don't want to pass work to them. For example, we're a design agency and if one of the people in the room is a printer that is rubbish, why would I want to pass on work? I'm not going to pass on work because I have to, because it's a reflection on my business.

So with partnerships, you need to be quite careful with who you're picking. I prefer to be selective and create my own strategic partnerships, choosing who we are working with. What's really good about this is that you can be really picky with who you want to work with, and only select someone who really complements your offerings.

An example might be that if you're an accountancy firm, you wouldn't want a partnership with another accountancy firm. Instead, a bookkeeper for an accountancy firm would probably be a very good one to partner with.

To ensure these partnerships are useful, I recommend that the company you're selecting as a partner should be of a similar size to your own. If you've got 20 people working for you, you don't want to start working with a one-man-band. They're not going to be able to pass you decent quality leads and the likelihood is you'll have very different views on price.

Another important rule is that you can't just be passing them work, it needs to work both ways. It's a two-way street after all and I always think that a strategic partnership should be of value to your clients too.

Going back to my example of the accountancy firm, you've now got bookkeeping covered. Perhaps think about IFA (an Independent Financial adviser). They would be great as they're focused on making your clients more money as well. So, if you can introduce your client to an IFA, it makes you look really good because you're trying to make them more money as well as save them money. Also, the IFA is getting more leads, so in return they can recommend their bigger clients to you.

Let's continue this idea. We might have an accountancy software firm, such as a Xero, KashFlow or Sage. You can partner with one of those, especially if they're really big. This gives people more reasons to want to work with you, because you can discount some software to make it more attractive to work with you.

Ok last example: A mortgage broker could also be a great partner for an accountancy firm. For anyone self-employed, we all know that it can be a struggle to get a mortgage, especially if you're only a year or two into your business. Wouldn't it be great if your accountant could recommend a mortgage broker that is used to working with self-employed people? Your clients would love the fact you're helping them and in turn you'll strengthen your bond with them.

To give you an idea of how Strafe Creative works, we are a design agency. We do graphic design, branding and web works, but we don't do SEO. We don't do any search engine optimisation, so we are linked with a company that just does SEO. We've linked with an SEO company which is great and we've also linked with a separate company that just does pay-per-click advertising, which includes Google adverts. So again, we can pass them lots of work but they also pass us work. We've also linked with a social media agency, so that any time a client wants social media work, I can recommend that company.

As I've mentioned, we want our partners to be the same size as us. So for us personally, we're looking for at least of 20 people in their team, if not more, because that's about the size we're at. As well as SEO, we're also linked to a hosting company. Obviously hosting comes hand-in-hand with web and vice versa. If they get big clients coming to them they can push email marketing, so again, it works well.

Other partnerships we've got are with PR agencies. We often get an e-commerce store that will mention that they've got big plans for the next year and need a PR agency to do so. Vica versa, we get lots of work from our PR agency partnership. They'll be asked to do some work on a site, but after looking through it, they realise no one can convert on it because it's poorly designed, so they'll introduce us before they start the PR campaign.

There are loads of complementary partnerships out there, you just have to think of how you can link with them and make sure they're non-competing but complementary. We've always made a list of all of our options and then we make sure we're happy with the partnership. Like I say, it's not just a one-way street. For example, if I pass a job onto a PR agency and later down the line they don't pass me anything, I'd just chase it up with them. If another period goes by where we don't get anything, we will break off the partnerships and we find a new agency.

We work with agencies that want to work with us, passes work, but, more importantly, also delivers a really good service to our clients, which make us look good. If that agency just passes us one job every three months, but we've got 10 partners, you can quickly see how easily this scales up. As long as you're delivering your side of the bargain then they're going to keep passing you work.

If anyone needs some help, if you're in an industry and just can't think how to do it, message me on Instagram on rossalexdavies. Mention: 'Strategic Partnership Help', tell me what you require, maybe even send me a link to your site, and I'll see how I can help guys.

21 BIG NUMBERS

This is all about using numbers to build credibility. As discussed in previous chapters, a great way to increase sales is to improve credibility and a great way to do that is by using large, impressive numbers. The great thing is, there are always big numbers to be found in everything we do day-to-day that will be impressive to others.

The reason these big numbers work so well is because of something called social proofing. As these large numbers are attached to your service and offering, credibility is automatically attached to you.

So let's use an example of a very small accountancy firm. They have only two members of staff and only 15 clients in total. But they work hard and aim to save their clients' money on tax. On average they save their clients £10,000 per year.

By combining these savings with their number of clients, you have the number £150,000. All of a sudden they have a big number to parade around! The accountancy firm can say "We saved our clients £150,000 last year, want to be one of them?"

Now that sounds impressive! Especially for such a small company!

Still unsure? Let's take an IT company. This time it's a sole trader with only five clients. All of his clients are estate agents with a few members of staff, but because of what they do, they send lots of emails every day. Let's say they send 100 emails a day. Over a year that's 36,500 and with 5 clients that's 182,500 emails per year!

Now, imagine if you were looking for an IT company to support your emails and you land on a website with a big title that said "We're so reliable that our clients sent 182,500 emails last year!". All of a sudden this one man band, looking after only five clients, appears super impressive and credible. Hopefully you're now starting to see how this can drive more sales into your company.

But what if I don't have any impressive numbers at all I hear you say? Well that's where big, bold, impressive goals come in. The example I use next is from a friend of mine called Marc Wileman, who runs Sublime Science. His big and scary goal when he set his company up was to make science awesome for one million children. Marc has been hugely successful and even went on to get backing from Dragons' Den. I hope you'll agree that having that lofty goal is impressive.

What excites me even more about this is that it's literally just a goal. When he set up his business, that was just his plan. It's a plan he mentioned in all of his marketing and it helped to build credibility with his potential clients. They knew he meant business and they knew he was wanting to build something different and special.

The main point of this chapter is that if you look hard enough, you will be able to find a big number or goal in your business. The credibility still works either way and that's what's so great about this hack. You can literally create a new goal, add it into your marketing, and overnight be a bigger and more credible company.

Let's finish with an option. You're after a web agency and you narrow it down to two companies. Both are super similar, their portfolios both look great, but one has a big goal saying "We want to generate £10 million in revenue for our clients". You'll probably go with that option as it seems credible, exciting, and you want to be part of that goal.

Think about your numbers and get something in your marketing right away, it's an easy one with big results!

Exercise:

- Break down what you do for a client on a monthly basis
- From these broken down tasks we now need to discuss the numbers attached to them, no matter how small.
- Or do you have a service (like the emails in this chapter) that, although you only do it a few times per month, allows you to create a bigger number for your clients than through their own actions?
- Multiply your chosen number by 12 to give you a yearly total.
- Once you have a number, multiply that by the number of clients you have.
- You now have your new and impressive number! But now you need to come up with a title which really gets this message across. Something simple which will be attractive to your clients.
- Get that message on all of your marketing!

P.s. Struggling with the numbers? Identify a number which sounds great to clients and use this as your goal instead!

22 UPSELL

This lesson is all about the upsell. But let's start with facts here: 20% of your customers will choose a more expensive option if you offer them one.

The mistake a lot of us service companies make is that we only offer one solution to our client and we do this for a great reason (or so we think!). The cost and service to that customer is bespoke to them. It's already tailored to their needs and we know it's perfect for them, so we don't bother to offer them anything on top of this. This is where we're all missing a trick! Imagine the amount of money we're all leaving on the table when 20% of our clients want to give us extra cash!

Now this in itself is a hack. In theory, it's an obvious one, but we're going to approach this from the tech industry point of view. We'll look at how they do this and the learnings we can take from this. A great example that I've seen is with the software Infusionsoft. It's a crm system and it's worth a look at. They offer a package where you get access to everything for a set price, but if you have any queries you have to go through email and there is a 24 hour wait. Alternatively, you can pay way more (the upsell!) and get access to someone directly. You can pick up the phone whenever you want. As their software is so expensive and powerful this extra is hugely valuable to the user and loads of people take up this option. Now essentially they are just willing to pay for better customer service, kind of mad really, but it really works!

This is where I think us guys in the service industry can really learn something from them. Personally, I think they've taken one of their biggest weaknesses and made it into an offer. Many of their clients had the software and loved it but struggled with sections and got fed up of having to wait around for answers. Clearly Infusionsoft knew this was an issue and offered to fix it if they paid more.

This works amazingly well for two reasons. It's a great way to better provide for your clients but also, if people do complain, you can push them onto this option, which in turn stops people complaining! It's blooming genius. They'll either pay more and love you, or be too cheap to pay more and not want to cause a scene so stop complaining. It's a win, win.

At my agency, Strafe Creative, the number one thing that people ask for is a super quick turnaround time. They'll have left it late or booked an event last minute and need something creating in time for it. Now this is always hard for us. As a general rule of thumb we book jobs around six weeks in advance. Of course there is room in there for movement and small jobs, but as a rule we're normally pretty booked up. So the only real way we can jump onto these bigger, quick turnaround jobs is with over time and moving projects around slightly. So, it's only fair that there is a hefty premium on this service. Just like Infusionsoft, we offer these clients two options:

1. We do this to our normal timetable and it will cost X.
2. We do this to your very short deadline but you must pay X (at 1.5 the rate).

As you can imagine, the extra cost isn't for everyone, but true to the start of this chapter, it's around 20% of people that take this. This is great for us as we've been paid 1.5% of what we would have charged. These clients also love it as we still get it done to their timescale.

Let's take another example of a solicitor. Imagine that your main offering is writing contracts for your clients. You have them on a retainer so that whenever they need anything new, they just call you up and you sort them out. But you discover that it annoys them when they call you up asking for advice and you charge them more. They see it as just advice but actually that's a part of your service, giving ace advice. So, instead of giving all of your advice away for free, you could create a premium offering where clients get unlimited time with you, as well as all the contracts they were already getting, plus a monthly meeting with you too.

This cost is five times what your standard option is. I bet that you get 20% of people sign up for it and, like I mentioned before, if people complain about the cost, then they don't get your advice. You can just point them to this option which in turn gets them to make their decision.

This leads nicely into having upsells at different times. When we do upsell we all have a habit of doing it only when we first provide a proposal. We should be offering some form of upsell to our clients at least once a quarter. It's great for you as it's much easier to sell to clients who you are already working with. It's great for them because as you start to understand their business more, you're able to provide even more value to them (at a cost of course!).

Now this next example is an idea I have which no one seems to offer. So if you're an estate agent, read closely. If you do decide to offer this service, let me know!

The standard option for an estate agent is to take photos of your house, take the measurements, and write a bio, putting it on all the major sites for you. Some will include showing people round the house as their standard service, some won't. They of course help with the legal bit of the purchasing too. But what if they had a really premium option? Imagine if you could have:

- A cleaner come to your house before every viewing to ensure the house is looking perfect before anyone steps through the door.
- A gardener coming once a week to ensure your garden looks amazing. They come every week until the house is sold.
- Fresh flowers are delivered weekly until the house is sold to give the rooms more colour and a beautiful smell.

- A handyman pops round before the first appointment to fix any small jobs around the house.
- Included in the cost is removal men to get you moved into your new house.
- Someone comes round and produces a full video tour of your house to make yours stand out from the crowd.

For anyone who's ever sold a house, they know that the extras I've just written would make a huge difference to the likelihood of a house being sold. It would make the entire experience so much nicer for you that most would gladly pay the extra % or flat fee that you would be charged for this service. You only need a small number of clients to take this offer up at a very high price for this to transform your business. This idea relates back to what I've mentioned before. An upsell is at its best when you're fixing a complaint for your industry. If you know something that people have a problem with, fix the issue then offer it to your clients at a premium rate. It's as simple as that.

Exercise:

- Hopefully a nice and easy practical for you now guys. Just follow the list and watch the magic happen!
- Make a list of your top 20 clients.
- Email them all asking this one simple questions: What is the one thing we could do to improve our service? (Title the email 'Bit of guidance please'). Good clients will want to help you and being asked for help is always nice.
- Collate the information and hopefully notice a trend.
- Plan out how you can fix this issue and come up with a premium cost for it.
- Go back to your clients and offer them the upsell.
- Email them thanking them for the extra cash!

WEB BASED

23 APPOINTMENT BOOKING

I've spoken a lot before about the purpose of a website and its main purpose, especially for the service industry, can be hard to pin down. We normally fall into the trap of just showcasing our services and hoping for the best.

Let's start off by explaining a really well-executed purpose on a website. Imagine that you're selling trainers online, the purpose is quite obvious. The purpose is to sell trainers quickly through your website. We want users to visit your site, find the shoes they like, select a size, and order it. Simple.

Not everyone is always going to be in a position to complete that set purpose. For example, they could be just looking around at the moment or waiting for payday. They might be unsure if those trainers will look right with their outfit. There's going to be thousands of reasons why people don't buy there and then and that's absolutely fine.

This is where a sub-purpose of a website comes in and that's normally around data collection. We want to grab users' details and give them something of value. Perhaps a coupon to get money off their trainers or some form of PDF that's going to help them, such 'How to keep your trainers looking white all year round'. The reason we give coupons away is so that we can build our database. We can then sell to that database whenever we have a new product or service to offer. If you have a big database, the world is your oyster!

Now we're all in the service industry, so it's highly likely that users aren't going to just land on our site and want to give us money. They won't just contact us to say "I want your service, let's get started!!". Sadly, the world doesn't work like that.

So, what purpose can a service industry website have? Whatever purpose we choose, we need to ensure it's fully trackable. This will ensure that we know if it's a success or not.

The best way to do this is by using KPI's, also known as key performance indicators, which can be properly tracked. You may have contact forms but there's aren't great KPI's as they don't give an accurate depiction of your conversion rate. This is because contact forms may be used by tire kickers and people who have no real interest in buying from you. Even worse, you might have people filling them in who are looking for jobs, or are recruitment companies trying to get you to sign up to their service. Just looking at the number of contacts coming in from a contact form is not a valid purpose for a site, as it's hard to track real, tangible leads.

An idea that we see working for clients a lot is to use an appointment booking software. The benefit of this is that you can put it directly into the site with a simple embed. The user can then select the date and time that they want to meet you, submitting their name, email, and phone number. What's really great is that all of a sudden this is fully trackable! We know that something is converting but we also know the identity of the prospects. We know that there won't be any tire kickers booking appointments, so there's only going to be strong leads.

The reason this works so well is that because it's an appointment, they're basically saying "Yes I'm interested in this". It forces the user to really think if they want an appointment. This is absolutely essential in getting more conversions of a high quality.

Now as you're reading this you're going to be arguing in your head and coming up with a list of excuses as to why this won't work. I bet they're along the lines of:

- I don't know what my diary is going to look like.
- What if they pick a date and the time that I can't do?
- What if they're really far away?
- I have lots of sales staff so this won't work for me.

Firstly, the appointment booking software links with all of your electronic diaries. Secondly, that's why you have their phone number from them. If you do have to ring them to change the meeting, it's not a big deal. It still forces the user to fully commit which is always the best option.

A great example of this is working with hairdressers. Potential customers can book a hair appointment to come straight into you. Likewise, some accountants give the option of a free review where a prospect can book straight in.

For my business, which is a design agency, we use this exact option and it's called our Project Planner. This is where people can fill in their details, note down their budget, and book in a time to speak to us. We use this system and it stops a lot of tire kickers, making the whole process a lot smoother.

Like I said at the start of this, once you've got a set purpose, it's actually trackable. Honestly guys, give it a try. It will transform your website from a brochure to something of value, which will show you tangible results.

There's loads of calendar software options out there which I won't list here in case they become out of date too quickly. Either give them a google or contact me on instagram at rossalexdavies with the subject title 'Help with appointment booking' and we'll send you our most up-to-date list. Good luck!

24 LIVE CHAT

When we first start working with a new client they always want quick wins and one of the best ways to do this is by installing a 'Live Chat' software. It's super simple to do and can make a huge difference to a business.

So what is Live Chat? Essentially, it's a bit of software which sits in the corner of your website and if someone wants to ask a question, they can click and speak to someone in your business straight away. It's perfect for people who are sitting on the fence and unsure if they want to move forwards with you. People don't really like picking up the phone, mainly because they feel that they will be sold to. Whereas live chat is seen as less personal and there is less danger for the user to get trapped into a sales funnel, so it's great for them.

It is possible to request an email from a user before you can chat to them. I would recommend not turning that feature on. My theory is that letting someone ask you a question shows that you care and that you can provide lots of value to them. In turn, this is likely to make them want to work with you. If you force them to give you an email first, yes you may build your marketing database, but if they didn't buy from you after speaking to you on Live Chat, they probably weren't the right person for your company anyway. Or even worst, they see that you're building your email database and decide not to ask you the question. They instead just close your website and don't speak to you!

Using Live Chat is all about providing value and being as helpful as possible. You may find that after a few questions you can then ask if they would like to book a meeting. All of a sudden you can see how easily this can drive conversions on your website.

We first started using this with e-commerce companies as before people purchased a product they may have had a quick question. We saw a huge spike in conversions and we've found that it's very much the same for service companies. From our experience, we've found that Live Chat can work even more effectively for service companies, because as a general rule of thumb, your offering is far more complex. This means that you're more likely to have questions that need answering.

Most Live Chat software has a 14 day free trial, so you can give them a go and see if you like using them. Most of them will plug directly into your website, so you may not even need a developer if you're using one of the common CMS programs, such as WordPress.
A couple of live chat options to try out are:

- Olark
- Live Chat
- Intercom

Try it for 14 days and see how you get on.

25 WEBSITE SLIDERS

This next lesson is a quick one. Although quick to explain and quick to execute, this can have a huge difference on your bottom line and the number of leads coming into your business.

This is very much a web tip and it's all about image sliders on the top of your site's page. When someone first lands on your page, that's called being 'above the fold'. It's actually an old newspaper term which refers to when big newspapers were sold. They were always folded in half when you bought them and the most interesting story was always above the fold, as that's what made you buy the paper.

That term is still used today for websites, as you want your most interesting content to be shown as soon as a user lands on the page. The common thing you see on at least 80% of websites is a big image slider with rotating images. The idea being that you can show lots of different information once someone lands on the page, or attempt to funnel people to different parts of your website. This simply doesn't work because as soon as someone lands on your page, they've only got two or three seconds to take in what you offer and decide if they want to stay on the site, or they just leave.

The mistake people make is that they may offer five different services, so they put five different sliders on there. They then expect the user to either wait or click through all of these. It's simply not the case. Think about when you visit a website. Do you just sit there and wait for the slider to rotate around? No, of course not. You continue down the page to look at other stuff, or worse, you leave the page because you think they don't offer the service that you're after.

There's loads of tests that prove this. The best results always come from focusing on your main value proposition to get users to stay on your site and investigate your services that way. Otherwise, it's just a pointless waste of space at the top of your homepage.

Let's put this into a quick example for you. Accountant A has a website with a slider which, like most other people, they put their four services on (one service on each slider). The sliders say:

- Quick and easy bookkeeping.
- PAYE and Tax services.
- Let us help with your end of year accounts.
- Financial planning services.

Their thought is that users will look at all of their services on the slider and click on the one which is relevant to them. But the likelihood is that they landed on the homepage, read the one about Bookkeeping, thought that was all the accountant offered, and left. Remember that you only have a few seconds to get across what you do and how you're different.

Now let's look at Accountant B. They don't have a slider. They instead have a big, clean title which is always on show, saying "Let us sort everything to do with your accounts so that you can focus on growing your business".

Which one are you likely to go with?... Exactly!

For people who ask 'why not combine the two?', there is one other reason not to use sliders. Having lots of large images which have to load the first time a user lands on your website can slow your site down considerably. This could not only ruin your Google rankings, but if your website is really slow, it's proven that people will just leave rather than wait.

You'll be surprised at the number of people and extra leads that you get from this simple change.

26 LANDING PAGES

So before we get into details, let's first explain what a landing page is. A landing page is a page on your website that is not accessible from the standard menu. It's only accessible if you send the user to this page. This may be through a Google advert, a Facebook advert, or even just direct mail. But unless the user is either told this address or sent there directly, they have no way of accessing this page.

The reason that it isn't accessible from a main menu is because you're going to put something on this landing page of real value. It may be a particular offer that you don't want the general public to have access to. You also want the user to have only two options when landing on these types of pages:

1. Perform the action you want them to (e.g: fill in a form or request a meeting).
2. Leave the page.

You do this by removing the main menu from this page so that the user can't get distracted. Ensure that all of the content on this page is convincing the user to perform the action you want them to. As the page is so rigid and the user only has these two options, it's a really great way to drive up conversions. Users are more willing to provide details when faced with such a black and white decision.

So let's put this into an example to better explain this theory.

Option 1: You have a blog post which sells a product at the bottom of it worth £1000. You then send 100 people to this blog post. Let's say you sell one product. Even though people were interested, a number of them started looking around your site instead and never went back to the product.

Option 2: You create a landing page with similar content to the blog post but it's more sales driven. The page has no menu, forcing the user to choose to either pay or leave the page. As they have to make that decision there and then you'll find your conversion is much higher, around three-four times higher normally.

The argument will be that 'this won't work for my industry', but you'll be surprised. Pitching the right service through a landing page can be huge for your business, especially if you already have some form of relationship with the person you're marketing too.

There are a couple of different bits of software that you can use for this. At Strafe Creative, we obviously build our own landing pages, but for people who don't have a developer and designer on hand, there are options such as Lander, Leadpages, or Instapages. There are also lots of plugins that you can use if you're using one of the standard CMS options.

But there are some sets of rules that we find work really well to build credibility and therefore increase conversions. Let's break these down:

- An obvious one to start with, but the page should have a title explaining what the user is there for. You have around five seconds for someone to decide if the page is relevant to them, so make the title obvious.
- Have a sub-title. A subtitle provides a bit more detail about what you're offering, which in turn keeps the user on the page longer.
- Videos work incredibly well on landing pages, even if it's just a talking head-style video with you explaining the offer. They feel more personal and drive engagement.
- This one is really more '3B'. It's worth testing if autoplay videos work for your target market. Autoplay means that as

soon as the user lands on the page the video starts to play. Certain demographics seem to like this and it can increase conversions. For others, it can stop anyone staying on your page and therefore you don't sell. You'll have to try both and see which one works for your target market.

- Avoid large blocks of text. People just won't read it. Instead, make use of bullet points as this will get across the same information but appears to the users as easier to digest.
- Have testimonials of people who have already bought them. See the testimonial chapter for more information on this.
- Use logo porn (again see the lesson on this).
- Give the user only one option and stick to your guns. If you want them to fill in a form, DON'T also give them a phone number. That gives the user too much choice which decreases the likelihood of them buying.

Good luck using this lesson and you'll be amazed at what landing pages can do for you.

27 404 PAGES

A 404 page is a page on your website that is shown when a user visits a URL that does not exist. It's an error page. If we take my website, strafecreative.co.uk and add /exampletest to the end of the URL, it will take the user to our 404 page. This is quite a common place for people to eventually visit, as they may have typed in something incorrectly or attempt to visit a link that is no longer there. Putting something of value on this page is a really great way of attracting more people into your database.

We have created a few different 404 pages in the past. We've created ones that had hidden raffles, in which users who found this page were asked to fill in their details to get access to our raffle. We've also created a 404 page which gave away special content, to make it appear like they had come across something special, rather they're just a standard error page. We find that trying to sell to users on 404 pages works really well. By offering the user something of value, we gain a larger database. This turns a useless error page into a platform to build your data, whilst offering the user valuable information.

You can also make these pages really fun and interesting for the user, so that they are more likely to get shared. On our site (or maybe old site depending on when you read this!), we used a comedic clip from Dumb and Dumber, which worked really well. People who stumbled across it would tweet us or like us on Facebook, or just get in touch to mention how funny they found it. There are many options with your 404 page and it takes minimal work to create, so it's worth trying it out.

28 THE LAST-MINUTE POP-UP

So the first thing to say is that I know pop ups are annoying! But damn do they work and as long as we're providing something of value to the user then I would argue that they aren't annoying, but actually super beneficial.

Now let's take the most obvious one that most people will have come across. It's the standard one that you see on online stores: "we will give 10 % off our product if you sign up." That's obviously a great one that works really well for e-commerce stores.

From a conversion point of view, with the e-commerce businesses that we work with, we find around 15% of all users will take up this offer. This is obviously awesome and something we all want to take advantage of. But the questions is, what can a service business give away? Now, the first thing I would say is don't give away a discount code. We're all selling our time in the service industry so the last thing we want to be doing is lower our costs and profits.

So to give you an idea of what we do at Strafe Creative, we do a last minute ditch attempt to say:

"Hey, why not get a free video web review of your website and see how you can improve it?" We get an 8% conversion on this, meaning out of 100 people that visit our site, 8 will fill this in. Which is great!

So there's loads of things you could do with this idea. Let's work through some more examples here:

You're a lawyer who might give away free terms and conditions for a website. It's generic enough that you only need to do it once but valuable enough that people would normally be willing to pay for it. The fact you're giving it away makes your company more attractive.

We have a client who does science parties for kids and they give away a little party pack experiment. The idea is that they can have a look at the experiment, like the idea, and then they are more likely to book a party with them.

The main aim of this is to give away something of value to your potential customers. Another great example is a music teacher who gave away free guitar plectrums. This offer helps identify the visitor as someone they can teach and it's valuable enough that someone would be willing to give you their details so that you can sell to them at a later date.

Now this pop up idea needs some software for it to work. The one that we personally use is called opt-in monster, which I love!

Now this software not only makes it easy for you guys to add these pop ups onto your site, but also allows you to select when the pop up appears. From experience, we find the best time is just as they are about the leave the page. The software realises the user's mouse is about to leave the website and it pops up. It's this last-ditch attempt which seems to really skyrocket the conversion rate and therefore your leads!

It's a little plugin too so if you've got a WordPress site, you can just plug it into the back-end so there's no coding needed for it. It then gives you little designs that you can have on the pop up, so there is really no excuse not to try this out straight away.

29 WISTIA VIDEO

This lesson is more about an awesome piece of software. I'm not linked with them but we use it religiously in my own business. It's for video marketing and it's quite a simple lesson really.

Most people seem to always use the standard video hosting platforms, the most famous one being YouTube. But there are loads of issues with this. For example, the adverts that play in it are annoying and at the end of the video Youtube will suggest other people's videos. It's not a great option if you're wanting to insert a video on your own website. Even the Youtube player is ugly and can't be personalised to look in-keeping with your own brand.

So the next option you'd normally see people use is Vimeo. Unfortunately, Vimeo is really only meant to be for non-commercial work. It's not meant to have anything business-related on it.

The one I recommend to all of our clients is Wistia. What's great about Wistia is that it fully tracks every single thing that goes on with that video. If you send it to one person, it will tell you if they watch it, how much of the video they watch, and if they pause it at any point. It also gives you information such as their IP address, so that you know the location from where they're viewing it. They can also tell you if it's been sent on to anywhere else. As soon as you start to use these analytics, you can get an idea of how interested viewers are. To put that into perspective, when we send videos out, we send them just to one person. It's always a custom video and I know that if they watch the video at least two or three times that they're very interested. I can then pick up the phone and call them. It's a simple hack but can make a real difference.

On the flip side of that, if they watch it once we might email them to remind them to watch it again or to see if they need to know more. You can see how knowing this extra information allows us to score them on how interested they are.

Now Wistia, at the time of writing this, is free for three videos, which should be enough for you to test if you want to use it. It's just a case of learning how to implement it, but if you can embed a YouTube video then you'll be able to embed a Wistia video.

The other great thing about it is that you can customise the colours and you can change how the player looks. If you want to have a big play button in the middle of the video, you can. If you want to remove the timeline to tell you how long the video is, you can. You can even auto play the videos as soon as someone lands on the page. It's a great bit of kit which is worth looking into.

Exercise:

- Go to Wistia.com.
- Set up an account and upload your videos to it.
- Replace any old videos on your site or marketing with Wistia versions.
- Leave them to build up data.
- View the data after a week or two and be amazed.
- For example, you may find out that on average, users are only watching 24 seconds of a £10k corporate video that you had done.

So once you know this you can get the video tweaked so people watch it all the way through.

30 PUSH NOTIFICATIONS

This lessons looks at what the tech companies are doing and how we can take advantage of it.

If you've downloaded any app you would have been asked if you would like to have the ability to push notifications to your phone. An example of this is with the taxi firm Uber. They request push notifications so that they can tell you when your taxi has arrived. It's a little pop-up that appears to tell you when something has happened.

This works really well in that industry, with more and more people using their phones to be notified for lots of different things. It works more successfully than an email, or being called or texted.

Now let's take this technology and use it in our service-based industries. Just as a note that unless you are sending something of value, do not use notifications. It's exactly the same as your email marketing. If you are constantly going to send content of no value or just to sell, then most people will ignore you. This is even more true with push notifications. If you're not pushing the right information then no one will listen, making it a redundant process. You'll just end up annoying people which we of course don't want to do!

With that in mind, we've used a couple of different softwares in the past. The first is pushcrew (pushcrew.com) and the other is called onesignal (onesignal.com). Both of these allow you to install a widget onto your website, asking users if they would like to be kept up to date with notifications of what's going on. This offers an even simpler way of getting someone to sign up for your email marketing. You can promote offers and deals, and all of a sudden, because they just get notified on their phones, they can click through on their mobile browser. It gets people to your site very quickly. Again, this works particularly well if you're offering the user something of value, something exclusive. If you're throwing lots of irrelevant, annoying things at them, it's not going to work. So, make sure that if you do decide to employ this technique, you are willing to give either discounts or offers.

There's lots of little things that you can do to provide push notifications of value. If you're an accountant, you could use push notifications to tell your clients when their tax returns are due. Or if you're a personal trainer, you could push a notification to ensure people are on track with their weight loss goals. There's loads of great ways this can be used.

You could use push notifications with Human Resources, notifying them to ask if they've got their contracts up to date. It brings this to the front of their mind, which you can then upsell on top of. It works so well because not many people are utilising these notifications at the moment, meaning it doesn't feel spammy or too obtrusive.

This is unlike email, which, a lot of the time, people aren't paying much attention to. I myself am constantly removing emails that I don't even read. But I do pay attention to a push notification, and I find them really useful. They're not amazing for everyone, and they can be slightly distracting, but I would definitely recommend trying it out. It's not expensive, perhaps £20 at month at most. If you get a couple of people to sign up then it pays for itself. So, give pushcrew or onesignal a go and let us know what you think of push notifications.

FOLLOW UP

31 FRONT OF MIND

This chapter is called 'front of mind' and the way best way I've seen this done is with none-sales lead 'touches'. The more personal and tailored they are to the client, the better. A great example of this is knowing your clients' birthdays. Think about a supplier that has sent you a birthday card, or even just a birthday email. I bet you can count that number on one hand. For the ones that you can remember, that's great, that's who we want to be! We want to be remembered as the suppliers that know our clients' birthdays, as it shows we care.

It's not as simple as just doing it for birthdays though. This is where we have to get creative and really get to know our clients. There will be some obvious ones like:

- Christmas
- Easter
- Birthdays
- Wedding anniversary
- Their kids' birthdays
- Birth of their children

But to really be memorable, we need to know what our clients love and then talk about that with them. An example could be that your client loves tennis. Email them about Wimbledon or an upcoming tennis competition, invite them to go to live games, or get them something tennis-related for their birthday.

Now the rule is that it MUST be sincere, genuine, and it can't be automated. You've got to put the time in and know your clients well. Big tech companies have the luxury of being able to ask all of these questions up front and then send you automated messages. It works, but for small businesses like us we need to take that to the next level.

Another example is that anyone who knows me knows I love basketball. I'm an avid follower of the NBA and if I'm not talking about design, I'm talking about basketball. So when suppliers make the effort to message me or get me things related to basketball I remember that. It forms a genuine bond with them and they're always at the front of our mind. If you can provide something like that to a client every month or so, they'll always have you front of mind, not just for you to help them, but for you to help their clients too.

This is where the CRM (client relationship management) software comes in. It allows you to make notes on all of your clients and as you add more and more information to it, you can use this to strengthen your relationships with them. It's essentially your database for all of the little things that you've learnt about them over the years. Even if you forget the information, it's still there if you ever need it.

Practical task:

Select your five best clients and write down everything you know about them; you want to list:

- Age
- Where they grew up
- Where they live now
- Married?
- Wedding anniversary
- Number of children?
- Kids' birthdays
- Sports
- Hobbies
- Car they drive

- Where they go on holiday
- Random facts you've learnt about them

If you don't know the answers, look on social media networks. There's usually a way of finding this out, even if it's just from recent photos of them doing things. Once you have this information, you'll then know the times to contact them. Remember to be genuine!! It's about building solid, genuine relationships so they like you and want to turn to you. It's not about getting money from them.

32 THE POWER OF QUESTIONNAIRES

Selling, in its broadest sense, is quite simple. You ask a client what the problem is, they tell you, then you offer to fix that problem for a price, simple right?

Actually it's scary that when you boil down to it, that's all we're doing. For example, I need a new car. So, I go looking for options and whoever offers me the best solution, I'll take it. Now this works no matter how complex the service or problem is. The car needs to have four doors, a big boot, be under a certain budget, with a good warranty. The potential customer gives you all of this information. They need to find the perfect solution and you just need to provide the best offering.

Sadly, car shopping isn't like buying a service. A potential client might have an idea of what they want, but rarely in detail. They know they want 'a car' but they don't know the spec.

So it's our job to delve into their reasoning as much as possible. This is also true for our current clients (the low hanging fruit!). That's what I'm mainly going to focus on in this chapter.

Questionnaires are great for two reasons:

1. You get an honest opinion of what people think of your business
2. You find out extra services that they need

Let's take my company as an example. We build websites that convert at high percentages. So after six months of a new website that we've created, we follow the client up. They inform us that the new site is converting at a really high percentage, but they want to grow so need more sales. So, their problem is traffic to their website. All of a sudden, we can offer them this extra service. It's a win for them as they get more people onto their website and it's a win for us as it's more sales!

Now go back to your clients, mention that you've noticed an issue, and offer your solution.

We don't send these questionnaires out all of the time, maybe once a quarter, if not less, but they're a great way to upsell clients onto more options.

Remember that these don't have to be done by email. You could instead have a quick call, or ask to pick someone's brains over lunch. The end goal is to find out whatever services they would find beneficial. That's not just for that one client, you could also offer that solution to your other clients too.

We had a recent client comment on the number of awards we had and how excited he was for us. After some back and forth, it was revealed that they had lost a number of tenders to one company who also had won a number of awards and felt these were adding credibility to their competitors. At Strafe Creative, we have a number of copywriters on staff and with the systems we have in place to enter awards, we're pretty good at writing applications too. So we offered this service to him, which he gladly accepted. But we then also created a quick marketing campaign and offered this service to a number of our other clients. The uptake was excellent and launched a new service that we had never considered before. This all came from asking the right questions and really listening to your clients.

We presume that all clients know every single service we offer, though you might find that after a questionnaire, they're having a problem that could be fixed by one of your other services. Even to this day, we have to constantly remind clients of all our services.

To track and get entries for our questionnaires, we simply use Google docs. There is an option to create a form to send to clients, which will then format all of the answers into a spreadsheet for you to better analysis. In this you can create multiple choice or opened-ended questions, whatever will provide you with the best feedback.

Let's finish with just a couple of questions you might want to ask. For a higher conversion rate on answers, don't ask more than three questions.

- Was the most recent project for you successful?
- How could we have improved?
- What's the one thing holding your business back from reaching your XXX goal?
- What could we do to help your business?
- Regarding XXXXX, are there any pain points in your current processes?

33 DISTRIBUTION

Distribution or giveaways is a great way to build your databases. For example, SAAS companies either give away their own software or other people's software which tie in to what they offer. This works well because they're offering their clients, their target market, something that they want. Typically, you can contact other companies and they will normally give you their software for free. I'm going to give you a couple of examples of where a couple of our clients have done this to build up their distribution list rapidly.

One of our clients was a brand new, independent gym, located near a lot of big well-know, corporate gyms, such as Virgin Active, David Lloyd, and Pure Gym. They wanted a giveaway that was going to be attractive to the type of clients they were trying to get. They spoke to a protein company called Myprotein and arranged for six months' worth of free products, worth between £400-£500, to be given to the winner of a competition. They advertised the huge protein pack and people had to sign up as a member, or trial the gym, to be in for the chance of winning it. Their gym got an extra 100 members signed up because of this deal. At £50 per month for membership, this really adds up.

Everyone's a winner here, because the prize is free, it doesn't cost the gym anything. They just had to advertise it. This independent gym has also created a relationship with a popular protein company. The protein company benefits from it because they're gaining free marketing, with more people wanting to buy their products after the competition is over. The No.1 winner is the client because they have access to win a great prize which they didn't have access to previously.

Another example comes from one of our clients which are an accountancy firm. In England, we have some accounting software that's really well-known, such as Sage, KashFlow, QuickBooks, and XERO. Our client approached all of them, wanting to offer their 50 clients free software memberships. The software company XERO said yes to this deal, in the hope that after a years' free membership, they would push these clients to stay on with them. So our client advertised this deal, encouraging prospects to sign up to gain this free gift for a year. As their target market was start-up businesses, this worked really well, because it saved them money as they were first setting up. Also, by 2018, taxes legally have to be done online, creating more of an incentive to take up this offer.

Our client gained 70+ new clients from this giveaway. It was a huge success for them. If XERO hadn't given them that deal, they would have had to pay around £25 per user per month for the same software, which really adds up (£21k!!).

If you'd like to do a giveaway to build a distribution list, then take advantage of someone else's credibility. It's a great opportunity for you to place yourself as a partner to a much bigger company. I recommend always partnering with a bigger company than yours so that, from a client's point of view, you're aligned with these big companies. These two smaller companies positioned themselves with national companies to give away free protein products and accounting software. So, have a think about how you can apply this lesson to your own options with distributions and giveaways.

34 BIRTHDAY CARDS

This leads on from the 'front of mind' lesson we've just discussed in a few chapters earlier. But this goes into more depth on how we approach birthdays. At the start of the year, go through Facebook, Twitter, and LinkedIn to try to find all of your clients and contacts' birthdays. Note these in a spreadsheet, along with their name and address, or potentially place of work. List them in order of birthdays and then you can begin to create a precise kind of business card.

Here at Strafe Creative, we've tested a few different versions out. We used to use a Strafe Creative-based birthday card, in which we'd write a standard message from our team and send it off to our clients. We also tried the Strafe branding with a more personal message inside. On our third version, we tried writing a personal message but on a standard birthday card, so that we weren't forcing our branding onto clients. As you can imagine, the best results came from the non-branded, non-sales birthday cards, which had a really personal message inside. This is because you've taken the time to find out when their birthday is; you went above and beyond other suppliers.

I've got friends who wouldn't even send me a birthday card, never mind clients! That's because nowadays you can use Facebook or email to wish people a happy birthday. Not many people send cards anymore. So going to the effort of doing this puts you at the front of your clients' mind.

It shows that you're caring, as you're not forcing your company down their neck with branding, and you appear personal. The other thing we find is that having a coloured envelope will always get through to the person. Doing this will make you stand out from the crowd.

At Strafe Creative, we have all of our clients' birthday in order of month. Once a month, I block some time out to write the cards all in one go, then send them out at the correct time. Personally, I prefer to write the cards because the card represents my relationship with a client. If it comes from someone else, it's not authentic. It's not good enough to just write "Jackie, Happy Birthday, from Ross and the Strafe team", as it defeats the objective of writing it!

Now, as your company gets larger, this can become potentially time-consuming and a bit costly, especially with the cost of buying individual cards and stamps. This is what puts a lot of people off doing this, which is the exact reason you should take advantage of it, to stand out. Even if you decide to just do this for your best clients or recurring clients, that's not a problem. However, we do this for all of our clients as it's a really nice way to show that we care and that we're thinking of them. It's an easy way to get back in touch and re-start a dialogue. It's all about staying at the front of people's mind so that they come back to you. A small bit of conversation can remind them of work they need doing which you can help them with. They begin to think of ways that they can utilise their relationship with you.

Lastly, the cards you buy should have a bit of personality to them, relating to your business. I try to buy quite funny cards, as that represents my humor. It's part of our branding that we don't take ourselves too seriously. You can have a card that subtly ties in with your brand without having your logo slapped across it. Also, as you can imagine, a card with your logo on isn't going to spend much time on someone's desk. However, a funny one might get shown around the office and will be left on a desk for a while.

ADVANCED

35 RECRUITER STYLE!

Every day we get absolutely loads of recruiters trying to contact us. Their usual approach will be to scan job boards to see who is advertising for certain roles. For example, my company might have an application out for a web designer or a web developer. If they're a company which specialise in web developers, they can contact us directly, because they know they have the solution to our problem. By solving it, they get paid. Whilst the calls are annoying, it makes total marketing sense, because they know exactly what I need before they've even spoken to me.

We can be doing this in our own businesses, but at the moment, not many people are! For example, if you are an accountancy firm, who also offers a bookkeeping service, look around for company advertisements asking for bookkeepers to join their team. You can contact this company directly to sell to them your booking service for a fraction of the cost of employing someone.

Another example might be if you're a HR Lawyer or HR solicitor and you see that a company is hiring for their first employee. You could contact them to ask if they want any help with this. Do they require employee contracts which you could provide?

We personally use this in web design. If we know a company is taking on more sales staff, we know that they are interested in sales and looking to grow. Therefore, we can offer to tweak their website to increase the number of leads that will come through it. It's as simple as scouring job boards for things that relate to your industry. Looking at job boards also allows you to build up a database very quickly to either contact or put in your sales funnel.

This recruiter method is successful because it's a great way to find direct emails or direct numbers for the heads of departments. They're willing to put their information on job boards. Occasionally, you will get a generic careers@ email, but a lot of the time you will find more direct contacts to use.

Also, jobs boards are a great secondary option to use as a search engine. This is great because you can find people who you may not come across just using Google. Using big search engines means you'll only find massive companies who are willing to invest in Search Engine Optimisation. If your company provides wood to builders or shop fitters, you can search for 'shop fitter' on Totaljobs to get a list of a thousand people whose companies are hiring. If they are hiring shop fitters, they probably need the furniture as well! Therefore, you can approach essentially a vast database of people in your industry, without having to buy any data or do an extensive Google search.

So do give this lesson a go guys. Unsure how this can work with your company or industry? Drop me a message on Instagram at rossalexdavies and I'll see if I can help!

36 GET A CRM

Now, in theory, this lesson should be a simple one. When we first set up Strafe Creative all those years ago, everyone told us to get a CRM system. But if I'm honest, it just felt like a lot of extra admin and I couldn't see the value in it. So this chapter is really here to hammer home the fact that if you don't have one yet (or don't know what one is) then it's time to get one set up!

So first of, what is a CRM? Well it stands for 'client relationship management' and it's software that records any interaction that you have with your clients or potential clients.

What's really useful, especially if you have got a growing team, is that you can see who's already liaising with who, or if anyone's been missed. Even if it's just you as a one-man band, you can start to see how many times you interact with certain clients, how many times you have to contact them during a project, and how many times you need to speak to someone before they actually want to work with you. The possibilities are endless.

It's all about tracking, because what you track, you can improve. You may have a team member's project which is running behind and they don't know why. But when you delve into the data that the CRM provides, you discover that they are contacting their clients only 50% as much as your other staff. Without that information, they can get away with blaming other things!

There are loads of options for CRMs, some of these include:

- Infusionsoft
- Hubspot CRM
- Microsoft Dynamics
- Sales Force

There are smaller options which do the basic job that you need them to do. The ones listed above are probably the most well-known ones in the CRM space and are far more advanced, maybe a little more than you might need to start with, but worth a look at.

A CRM should track every interaction, so emails are normally automatically inserted. However, you'll need to manually enter phone calls, meetings, and webinars (etc) but it's worth it. Some of the more complex CRM systems will be able to link into your website so that, if you send an email and a user clicks on the link in the email, it will tell you what pages they are viewing on the site. All of this information can then be used to provide a more personalised service to them.

I'm not going to lie to you, they are a pain set up. But there are a few important things you can do to make it run more smoothly.

Get an Excel spreadsheet together of all your contacts. Have them split by first name, second name, email, company, and telephone, as well as any other relevant information you may have. If you're using Gmail or Outlook for your emails, you can just export all of your contacts with a click of a button. You'll just need to tidy up the data before you insert it in.

A CRM is a great piece of technology but it's only as useful as the data you insert into it. If the data you insert is messy, or worse, you don't update it, then you won't see much value in using it. Be consistent and as detailed as possible. You never know when you might need to go back in time and look through the archives for information.

Get all of your staff onboard and have a defined way of filling in the system. If you just allow everyone to use the CRM in their own way then the data will have holes in it. Create a process and force staff to stick to it. It may not be the way they are used to, but it will mean everyone knows exactly where to find information when they need it.

The other good thing with CRMs is that you can monitor the pipeline of your sales. Every time someone comes in as a basic lead, you can put them in there and then push them through your funnel. For example, if someone goes from a basic lead to a qualified lead, you can move them along in a visual manner, using your CRM. For someone like myself, who likes everything visual, it's a great way to work.

As your sales funnel will be in here, you could also start to see if there are any sections of your funnel which fall down. The CRM will note at what point a lead becomes dead. The better CRM's in the market will also allow you to record the reasons that you lost a sale, which over time will allow you to analyse these reasons. We all think we know the reason and we make excuses, but most of the time what's in black and white is always the option to go with.

The hope with this book is that you will have so many leads that you won't know what to do with yourself (that's the dream!!). But, if you are getting lots of leads but you can't even convert them into a meeting, what are you doing wrong? Are you coming across as rude on the phone? Are you not following up quickly enough? Is there something in your proposal that's putting people off? That's why you need to have a CRM. It's the knowledge and the power of that knowledge which is vital to any successful, growing business.

37 LOVE GOOGLE ANALYTICS

This lesson is about learning to love Google Analytics. It's a feature by Google which provides analytical software that you can plug into your site for free. It will tell you about the users visiting your site, including what pages they visit, the order they visit them in, where they have come from, how long they spend on your site, and what pages they leave on.

It's a really powerful tool, the No.1 tool that is utterly under-utilised by most companies. Most people install it onto their website and just look at it every six months to check if they have more traffic.

There are a couple of areas in Google Analytics which we think are absolutely key and what all the big tech firms are obsessed with. These are:

Behaviour Flow:

This feature is useful because it tells you, on average, how most people move through the first five pages of your website. You'll be able to see the first pages they enter the site on, and where they go next. Every industry is different so it's interesting to see the different user-behaviour flows. Some industries' target markets will go straight to the Services page. Other might go straight to the Case Studies, viewing previous projects that have been done. Some may want to go to the About page to learn about the team behind a project.

Every company we work with is slightly different. It's important to look at Analytics first, because it tells you what people want to know before they work with you. You can also see how clear your site's design is, by examining how people navigate around it. You may even find out that pages that you think are really important are actually totally overlooked by the users. So, this is either because it's not important to them, or it's not easy to find.

Goals:

Make sure you have some form of goals set up. These can be as simple as getting users to visit a certain page, or more importantly, getting someone to fill in a contact form or pick up your phone number. You can track this by having an analytics code which is attached to the phone number on your site. It will track all the times this number is called. You can choose the source that this number comes from. If the number comes from Google Ads, it will have a different code to if the number was found organically. You can then find out why people are ringing that particular number.

Also, for contact forms, you can add triggers so that every submitted contact form gets registered in Google Analytics.

Any type of contact on your site should be set up in Analytics. Once you have goals, you're able to track back and see where the traffic is coming from. You can also track people coming from social media, learning which platforms lead to prospects contacting you, and which platforms need more money or time invested into them.

It's vital that you get your Analytics set up early. In theory, any piece of marketing that you have will funnel your prospects to your website first, to help them get in touch with you. This is what all the big companies are doing. They're using Analytics to spend their money smarter. There are far too many small companies who try many ideas to see which ones work. If they took a step back to look at their Analytics, they'd be able to see where their money is being used, and invest in the successes and not in areas which aren't working.

38 GMAIL ADS

Now this might sound like a weird one, but it's about Gmail advertising. Gmail and Gsuite are names of the email clients from Google. With Gmail being the most popular email client in the world, it's a great place to advertise your service in a different way to the norm.

If you've ever used Gmail; you'll know that the top email is normally an advert and you can appear here!

Gmail advertising is always overlooked as an advertising platform. It is part of the pay-per-click system but the best way to run these is selecting to only appear on Gmail adverts. As we're only running the ads on Gmail, the price is tiny and very cost-effective.

I've seen thousands of these adverts over the years and most companies suck at this. They just throw it in as part of the usual Google PPC marketing, where it's best used on its own. We find that the best way to use Gmail ads is to relate them to what a user will have in their mailbox at the exact time of seeing the advert.

Let's use an example here of a trusty accountant! Now in the UK, the end of the tax year is April. The likelihood is that smaller companies, whose MD is still involved with their finances, will be emailing back and forth with their current accountant. Let's says it's not going smoothly, or worst, the accountant has messed up or forgotten something. You're emailing them to try to sort this issue out.

All of a sudden, surprise! Your Gmail advert pops up saying either "Hey there, behind on your payments or not happy with your current accountant?" or, "Let us sort the tax man for you!".

The reason these type of adverts work so well in Gmail ads is because the potential customer is already thinking about their accounts and the problems they're having. For the right person, your Gmail advert is perfectly timed!

Personally, we've always seen that the best use of Gmail adverts is very targeted to a set group of people and normally relates to something around that time of the year.

It must be noted that the click rate on this will be tiny, less that 1%. But, if you're really targeted, the people that actually do click on it will be genuinely interested in your offering.

39 COLD EMAILING

Now, cold emails aren't to everyone's liking and to be honest I'm not a huge fan of them, but that's mainly because most people do them badly! Everyone always says "Oh, I get those emails every day and I never bother to read any!". I'm telling you now, that's a lie. What you mean to say is that you probably don't read 99% of them but you will always read at least one of them, won't you?

And that is all we need. That's all cold emailing is, a numbers game. So, if I send out 100, I need one person to read that and get back in touch with me and it's all worth it.

Now, you need to obviously do this at scale. For example, you can't use your standard email client (e.g. Outlook) and start firing out emails on mass. It's just not built for that and you'd be there all day.

Let's run you through a standard process:

- Select the market you're after.
- Provide filters on what you're after too, eg: size of business, job title you want to speak to, turnover of business.

As we're a web agency, once we get these lists, we then manually check each website and look for the rubbish ones or the ones we could improve dramatically. The value I'm going to be providing to these people is that my team can increase the number of sales and leads their website is generating.
We have our processes in place so that we work on the basis that for

every 150 emails we send, we get one really good lead. We average around 12 responses from those 150, but normally only one of those is strong enough.

So, let's then do the numbers from here. If I buy data of 5000 companies, I should get 33 really strong leads (as a minimum for us).

This hack alone could transform your service industry, as I'm sure most of you reading this don't get 30+ strong leads a month. Imagine the growth that your business could see with those kind of figures?

There is a couple of rules of thumb that you need to know and follow religiously though. The first one is that if you just send one email, you will make no sales at all.

In our system, we send seven emails at a minimum, as no one buys on the first try. Obviously, please do not send these back-to-back because that's just annoying and they will delete them. Instead, we send seven over a period of two weeks, which might seem intense, but we find this is the sweet spot and continues to work for us effectively.

You need to space out these so that they don't look automated as well. For example, after the first one, wait two days to then send another one. Send the one after that three days later. The main idea is to keep them spaced out but varied.

When we send out these cold emails, we try to cover all of the different potential personalities. For example, one might be an introductory email just on the off-chance that they read it. Another might talk about how good we are and what we've done. These will attract the type of person that's interested in growing their business. But then we'll also do an email with a subject about them missing out, because fear tactics work really well for cold emails as well. We normally have one email just showcasing happy client testimonials, as a way to build credibility too.

We always finish our seven emails with one that we like to call the 'Golden email'. It's super simple and pretty much just says: "Are you okay?" or another version you can send is "Have we offended you?".

You'll be surprised at how many people open this and respond. I think it's because it genuinely feels like you care, it feels more personal and you do find you get a lot more responses. Some people will respond with a "No, don't worry" type email and I would always say this is better than nothing. It opens up the dialogue between the two of you and at least they're interacting with you now, which is better than before, as at least they know who you are now! You never know, something might come from that interaction at a later point, so for me, cold emailing is a no brainer.

There are another couple of important rules to follow. Don't send lots of emails per day as this can affect your email sender score. In turn, this can cause even your normal emails to end up in the spam folder. So that's a big no, no.

An effective system to use instead is to make use of a subdomain in your emails. You'll see all the top email companies doing this. As they're using a sub-domain, it protects the normal address, so even if that one ends up blocked, they can just switch to another subdomain. Imagine that your current email looks like:

ross@example.com

You should be sending all of your cold emails from: ross@e.example.com. You'll need your IT company to set this up, but once done you at least know you'll never have an issue with spam filters.

I mentioned at the start of this lesson that you can't use your standard email client. The option we've found that works really well is replyapp.io. Now, the clever reason we like to use this is because, not only can it automate the sending out process, but it's also got a smart system built into it.

So, after the first email, if they don't reply to it, it will send the next one in the chain. But the really clever bit is, when they do reply, the system knows to switch off the automated approach and funnels the reply to your main email. This way, you can respond personally, which in turn makes it easier to convert this cold lead into a hot one.

Next rule of thumb is that I try not to send out more than 100 cold emails in a day. I know that I've already explained about the subdomain option, but one can ever be too careful. It's also a pain to have to switch subdomains a lot.

The next rule is an important one. People seem to think that email marketing, even cold email marketing, should have lots of images and be fancy. This is the easiest way to end up in someone's spam filter. It's super obvious that this isn't a personal message to them, it's clearly mass market. So another reason I love replyapp.io is that they all look like standard emails. On first glance, the user will hopefully think it's personal to them, rather than for a mass market.

This leads me nicely into my last rule. Use varied signatures in your cold emails. It's a great way to seem more personal, as if you have just thought about them there and then. What I mean by this is, in the first email you may use your standard email signature, but in the next one you might change the signature to say 'Sent to my iPhone'. It feels like you've taken the time to get in touch with them whilst on the road.

Looking personal and un-automated is going to be super important in ensuring people actually reply to you. Try to vary these up and make sure the emails are chatty and inviting, rather than the standard, overly-professional ones that people normally receive.

Cold emails are probably one of the first things that we did at Strafe Creative which really started to grow our business. As we created it as a system, it was a bit likes a sales tap. If we were a little quiet, or needed to drum up sales for a new staff member, we could turn this on and drive in new sales. This in turn works the other way around as well. If you're too busy, you can stop sending them out. It's a win, win!

Whoever you use to purchase your data, try to get an account manager, as they'll start to understand the type of data that you really want. They'll get used to filtering and cleansing the data in the way that you want it provided.

Any questions on data purchasing, just message me on Instagram at rossalexdavies. Good luck!

40 HIDING RETARGETING

This chapter is all about Retargeting, a hack that we've previously discussed in this book. Just as a reminder, Retargeting is when someone is repeatedly exposed to your company and your marketing methods. For example, someone can visit your website and the little pixel on the side of your site tracks this person's visit, taking in to account when they leave the site too. After visiting, they are re-shown your company's banners and other marketing items to become more aware of who you are.

This is a great idea because anyone that visits your site is reminded of you later on. It keeps putting your name out there and spreads awareness of your company.

Another thing you can do is choose how long someone has to be on your site before you start tracking them. For example, you can set it so that your tracking doesn't load until someone has been on your site for 30 seconds or more. In theory, after this amount of time, the people on your site will be far more interested in your company and your retargeting. With standard retargeting, you could potentially be wasting money on people who only visit your site for a couple of seconds and then leave straight away, so this way you know you'll only be spending money on interested people.

It's not a simple thing to set up, so show this chapter to your developers and they'll be able to sort this for you. To give you an idea of cost saving, we cut our retargeting spend by about 40% from doing this, with the same amount of leads. So for the bit of extra work, it will pay for itself really quickly.

So this is just another potential hack that you guys can do to decrease the amount of money you spend on the wrong sort of people.

41 REPURPOSE CONTENT

There needs to be a warning at the start of this lesson and that it's you already need to be creating content for this to work! The idea of repurposing is exactly as it sounds. If you've created something of value (for example a blog post) once you've created that item of value, you should be getting the message out there in as many different ways as you can, on as many different platforms as possible.

Let's take this lesson that you're reading right now as an example. I could record this and have this as a podcast, or speak to a camera and put it on Youtube. I could flesh it out with imagery and it could be a blog post. Using Powerpoint, I could turn it into a short presentation and put it on a website such as slideshare.

You'll see from just this short lesson that there are lots of different ways this content could be consumed.

The great thing about this is that you don't have to be constantly coming up with new bits of value to get in touch with your potential customers. As every person likes to consume information in different ways, the likelihood is that that they won't realise that the content has been shown before.

The system I use is a simple spread-sheet. I normally always start it as a written piece, but that's just me, everyone is different.

Once the content is written, I then use the spreadsheet and mark off as I change the content to be repurposed. Not every single thing that you do can be repurposed into ten different options, but at least if you're tracking on a spreadsheet you know which items work well in the different media.

So to give you an idea of ways that you can present your content in different ways to repurpose it, check out these:

- Blog post
- Guest blog post (slightly re-written)
- Talking head video (on either Facebook or Youtube)
- Infographic video (on either Facebook or Youtube)
- A quote from it as an Instagram post
- Presentation on slideshare
- Presentation for a course
- Downloadable PDF for growing your database
- Infographic for Twitter and Facebook
- Podcast
- Part of a webinar lesson
- LinkedIn post in a group
- Facebook post in a private group
- Book Chapter
- PR release
- Blog comment on other companies' blogs
- Live video on Periscope, Snapchat or Instagram stories
- Email marketing

Exercise:

Take a blog post (or write something your customers would find of value) and choose three ways you could repurpose it and do it!

Now, it doesn't need to be perfect, you just need to do it! You'll perfect them as you go, so don't worry if your videos aren't perfect to start with. It's more important to just start them and give it a go!!

42 DOWN SELL ON LEAVE

Now anyone who knows anything about selling already knows this, but wait a moment, as we're coming at this from a tech point of view. We're going to look at how the big tech firms are using this to growth hack their company's profits, then take the lessons from this to come at this idea from another point of view. For people who haven't used this before, it essentially works like this:

Offer your option and then, if they can't afford it, offer them a different solution at the budget they can afford. Yes, it's not the perfect solution but it's a win, win for everyone involved.

What tech firms, who are operating online, are able to test quickly, is what type of down sell works best. As their entire customer journey is online, they're able to know the best possible time to offer the down sell and what that offer and price is. So since they've done all of the work, it only makes sense that we take advantage of this!

What's interesting to note is that tech and software companies do this best when you're leaving their company. It's that moment when you go to close your account down with them that they hit you with the great down sell. What they can do, which is really clever, is because the software you're using is all tracked, they can see what offer they should provide you based on your usage.

Let's take an example I came across. I was using some software which was £200 per month and provided five tools as part of it. After about seven months we realised we were only regularly using one of the tools and could get that one tool from a different bit of software much, much cheaper. So, we went to close our account. Boom, the software says "no please don't go! We notice you mainly only use this tool, why not just pay us £40 a month and just have that?". How awesome is that!? As this down sell isn't available on the main site, it's only an offer to keep you as a customer at that exact point and it's brilliant.

We've all lost clients over the years who need to save money, looking for cheaper alternatives. Our usual option is to wave them off and go find more clients. But what if, when they go to leave, we look at what services you actually provided them and offer them just that one part of the service at a certain price? You'll be surprised at how often this is picked up.

Let's apply this to an example in the service industry. You run an IT firm and charge your clients to look after their computers, their internet, and their emails. You charge them £1000 per month to look after their 20 computers. They recently asked you to help purchase all new computers and then after five months of the new computers you get a call to say that they're having to terminate your contract. It's not that you did anything wrong but they're looking to save money. You can either:

1. Say no worries, be nice and wish them good luck, and of course kiss goodbye to that nice retainer.
2. Look at what you've actually been doing for them since the new computers were fitted. You notice that actually, since they're running brand new computers and invested in great kit, you haven't done a single call out for them and currently you only handle their weekly email issues.

You should be going with the B option all day long! As we now know, they weren't getting value from your service, hence why they're now looking for a cheaper cost.

So work out how much your offer would be to just provide that one service and then go back to them.

The main thing to remember with this option is that we're not discounting our costs. Discounting is the quickest way to go broke. Instead, we're just re-evaluating our offering to ensure they're still a client. Eventually, when those shiny new computers do start to wear and need updating, they're still employing you and want you back to your full service!

I'd personally rather still have them as a client, just at a lesser cost. But, be careful, don't do anything extra for free or they'll hold you to it. If you reduce your service to match a budget, ensure that they know when you need to go above that budget, to do any extra work. You'll have them back up in no time!

43 EXCLUSIVITY

This lesson is about exclusivity, aimed at those who are trying to get into a premium market and out of the 'budget' range. Appearing more exclusive is a great way to drive people to get in touch with you, especially the better, more targeted leads.

A famous example of this is a company called "Secret Escapes", who offer holidays. Rather than a standard holiday website, where you can submit your price range and location and then find a holiday, Secret Escapes is much more exclusive. You have to become a member of their Secret Escapes Club, giving them your details, before you can even begin to view holidays. This is a great way to not only build your database, (having contacts who you can sell to at a later date), but to send out the point that you're desirable and special and that not everyone has access to you.

A business coach that we know very well applied this idea to his website. On it, he explains what he does but that he is very particular with who he works with. He requests that anyone who wants to contact him must fill in a criteria questionnaire first. This makes people evaluate if they're ready to contact him, meaning the leads that do come through are good quality and are more willing to invest their time into him. It means that he's not wasting his time with tire kickers either.

Another example is a personal trainer who runs a very similar scheme in Leicester. He has an application form on his site and has 10 commandments. The 10 commandments state what he expects of everyone who he works with and to be honest, if you did those 10 commandments without his help, you would be really fit anyway! As the way they are written will only attract people who are deadly serious about getting into shape and are driven enough to see it through. As he is making people apply as well, it automatically gives him that air of importance, that he isn't willing to just work with anyone.

If you're just looking to get in shape a bit, with a casual commitment, then this PT isn't for you. They're targeting people who really want to add on muscle or train for an event. It's really putting off certain people, meaning the people that come through their site are more targeted and qualified. It makes selling to the right people much easier.

A lot of tech companies are using the same idea, designing their site to be more exclusive. They're targeting their market much more through their design, which will only put the people off who they didn't really want in the first place. It means their leads are much more ready to buy when the time comes to it.

Another example is of a furniture shop that used to be in Nottingham. It was an invite-only furniture shop, in which you had to either be invited or request an invitation before you could even walk through the door. Although that might seem weird, it stops people casually dropping in who were just passing. It means that the people who enter have taken the time to look through their site, its products, their prices, and were willing to book an appointment. It means the people who enter the shop are really interested in buying.

There's loads of examples that you can relate to which can help you to massively increase your profits.

Exclusivity might not just help you in terms of making more money overall, but it might also help you get qualified leads. You won't have to waste your time with the tire kickers, the people who were never going to buy from you in the first place. So try some of these ideas to see how being more exclusive can massively help you.

44 RETENTION RATE

A SAAS (software-as-a-service) business breaks up its marketing into different sections. Obviously one of them is acquisition, trying to get as many new people to their website and signing up as possible. But because of how quickly the software industry moves, they also focus on their retention rate. They'll look at their churn rate, (how long a client stays with them), to compare it against how much they spent to fill their marketing pipeline. SAAS companies try to optimise their retention rate, which is important for any business.

An example of this is with Twitter. Twitter discovered that when people first sign up for Twitter, they may not be particularly tech savvy and know how to use it. Twitter found that the quicker someone got to following 30 people, the higher the retention rate. So they have tweaked their sign-up software to get you to follow 30 people as quickly as possible. It now links with your friends list from Facebook and Instagram and gives you recommendations of relevant things to follow. This helps them increase their retention rate.

In our own service businesses, I think we make the mistake of looking after a client for a while, leaving them be, then moving on to the next one. Actually, we need to have systems in place to analyse why people like to stay with us. Probably the best way to do this is through some form of a questionnaire, which I've mentioned in other lessons. You should keep in contact with them, maybe go for a coffee to see where you are with each other. Is there anything that you could be upselling to them? Once a client is already with you, they are far more likely to spend with you again. So, look at the extra things that you can offer them to increase your retention rate.

I said before that service companies are bad at doing this. We had a HR company which we mainly used for contracts and occasional help with issues. They were our cheap option when we first started up. They never really provided any form of service but at the same time we never really needed them for anything. Therefore, we didn't keep in contact with them, we just paid our monthly fee and viewed it like we view insurance. It was only once the business started to grow that we required more from them. I met some other HR professionals who told me what they were doing for their current clients, such as visiting their business for reviews, sending newsletters to describe things that were changing in the law, and sending clients diaries to monitor people. So I switched to them. From our old HR company's point of view, we never asked for anything. We service companies have the habit of thinking that because we've not heard from a client, everything is going well.

We need to be constantly keeping in touch with clients and seeing if we can help them. The easiest one to try is to send something of value to them every month, whether that's through an email, text, or quick phone call. The more value you can give them, the more likely they are to retain with you. What you offer may be as small as seeing something on a website that might be of use to them. It's simple but can massively increase your retention rates.

45 LEVELS OF SERVICE

Have you ever noticed that online software do a great job of giving you different options of what you might want to purchase. There will be the cheap option, which offers perhaps two or three things. The next option up may cost more and might provide you with four to five more things. Then there is the premium option, which includes the complete package of everything that the software can possible do.

Essentially, they are providing costs that any person can afford. We don't do this enough in the service industry. Someone may come along and want something far simpler than what we offer and want to do. I never believe that we should give discounts because this just narrows your profit margin. Instead, we can provide them with a simpler, reduced service to make the price cheaper. It's similar to when you buy a car. There will be a top of the range version that costs a lot a month. But if we take the version without the leather seats, removing those little add-ons can reduce your monthly price. It's the same with our business. If we can offer levels of service as options to our customers, they can make the decision themselves. You need to establish that they won't receive the same amount of service but that you can still help them.

I think having that agreement at the start of a project really helps. This is because a lot of service companies provide discounts, which devalues the service and means they don't want to do the same amount of work anymore; they know they're not getting paid what they should for a job.

So we can come up with options where, for a slightly lesser service, a client can pay less. For example, your standard accountant option provides the yearly books, as well as the personal tax returns for the directors and bookkeeping. If someone wanted to reduce their bill, you could remove the bookkeeping and personal tax options to just focus on the business bit. This example shows that, even in the service industry, you can cut packages down to make them cheaper. This doesn't mean that you can't upsell them at a later point, but it's about helping your clients get onto that first step with you. I think service companies have a tendency to stick to flat fees and set packages, but make sure that you can provide an option for every potential client.

46 SHORTEN THE CUSTOMER JOURNEY

This lesson is taken from a great example that I've seen recently on an ecommerce store. Just a reminder, an ecommerce store is an online shop and refers to any place where you can buy online. The example I've seen recently is using Apple pay, where you can buy anything with your fingerprint on iPhone's (android have their own version too). If you choose Apple pay, your thumbprint does the job of your bank card. This is a really great way of showing how software service or e-commerce stores are drastically reducing their customer journey, from 'interested' to 'buy'. No need to enter card details or delivery address, just put your thumb on it and your registered card and address are already in the system, it's amazing!

We service industries also need to think about what technology we could use to simplify our processes. We are all guilty of making some processes unnecessarily long. Here's an example of something we used to do at Strafe Creative:

Someone would ring and ask for us to price-up a project. As everything we offer is bespoke, we felt that we needed to meet this prospect in person for an hour to establish the project and brief. We'd then write up everything discussed and send them a spec (not a cost, literally just the spec of what we discussed) which felt like we were over-delivering to them. We thought giving more information would be appealing to a prospect and felt like we really understood what they were after. We'd ask for them to confirm the spec and to add anything extra to it, which would add two-three days to the proposal stage. Once they'd sent the confirmed spec back, we would write out the proposal, a lengthy document covering all jobs and costs. We'd then organise a phone call for a few days later to find out whether the prospect rejected or accepted our proposal. As you can see, even the initial proposal stage lasted between two-three weeks. Which when I look back, was a crazy way to do things! Though I'm sure there's many of you reading this that are currently doing something very similar.

Now we have a slightly different approach. If someone contacts us for a job, we provide them with an initial kind of questionnaire which divides up those who are just shopping around for prices from those who are looking for something more detailed. Those who require prices only need 10 minutes on the phone to have a discussion about their project plans and for us to provide them with rough costs. We've found that being honest about needing time to quote on exact costs works well with prospects. As you can see, the first stage of their customer journey has been reduced from two to three-week to 10 minutes. The rate of people who have come back to us is now much higher. I think that the service industry can feel worried that we need to spend a while with a prospect and gather as much detail as possible to understand them. Whilst this of course has a place, this does not have to happen for every quotation.

The other type of customer to identify is one that requires more detail from us. This type will have a meeting in which we'll fill in a questionnaire to establish the full spec there and then. This spec can then be sent to the office to slot into the proposal in a streamlined fashion. In the meeting, we'll organise a proposal phone call for a day or two later to receive immediate feedback on it and potentially move forwards with the job. A lot of clients actually need asking if they want to move forwards with a job. We all have a habit, especially in England, of feeling worried about pressuring prospects. Don't see it as pressure, but more as offering them the chance to move forwards if they wish to. If they need more time to look over the proposal, we can just reschedule the appointment slightly. As you can see, this process takes two to three days rather than two to three weeks. It's cutting down these little things that makes a big difference.

The last note, that also ties into this stage, is about getting your Terms and Conditions signed. These would usually have to be printed out, signed, scanned, and sent back to us. This is time-consuming. We now use an Adobe feature called "EchoSign" to send over the proposal, which gives the prospect the option of signing with their mouse or typing out their name as a legally binding document. Again, if this was manual and having to be done by post it would take ages, even just emailing it, having them to print, sign and scan back is time consuming, But using Echosign has turned it into a ten second job.

I think all service industries could benefit from shortening their customer journey. It really does make a big difference. See how you could potentially shorten yours by trialing some things. If you manage to find your version of "Apple Pay", do drop me a line on my Instagram at rossalexdavies, as I'd love to hear what you've done.

47 PICKING A HOTEL

As I'm writing this, it has become apparent to me that a lot of my learnings of what I do are based around food and restaurants. I'd like to apologise that there are a number of these in this book, but there's another important lesson that we're going to take from this, which is why it's been included.

For a little bit of background, I like to go surfing, so I visit Wales as much as possible. My family and I stayed in a place called Llandudno, which I had never been before, because we were going to Snowdonia, (which has a man-made wave where you can surf on it.) Llandudno is a very beautiful seaside town and is very much an up-and-coming town as I write this. This is what we found:

We were staying in a very nice hotel along the sea front, which was around a mile long. All the buildings were essentially the same, all tiered and beautiful looking Victorian houses. I would say 99.9% of them were hotels. Every single one of them had a restaurant and a bar. Now the problem you have got from a marketing point of view is: How do you appear differently?
They're all in the exact same sector and they all have the same architecture, though on slightly different pricing levels. Some of them were really cheap, such as £35 per night which is unbelievable, but they are all essentially serving the same thing. The tough things was that we were trying to find somewhere to eat but there wasn't really anywhere on Trip Advisor and your hotel tries to push you to eat in their on-site restaurant.

Actually, that's not really how most people work nowadays. You don't necessarily want to be in your hotel for all of the night. You want to go around and try some food and experience different things. However, because everyone was doing the same thing, no one stood out from the rest. Even though the hotels were really nice, the hotel restaurants were not doing anything different to all of the other ones. There are hundreds of these restaurants that serve the same type of thing.

We found one place that had taken an old hotel and turned it into a restaurant, going to town on making it really different. It was all about the seafood, niching it down, looking at the whole market. This restaurant had made itself special and really different to what the rest of their market did. It had a fancy bar to start the night, a stunning, very differently styled main restaurant from most, a smaller private room for big parties to hire, and a second, more relaxed bar as well. Although this place ,in any other town, would be the norm, no one else in the area had done this. All of them had a hotel and a restaurant, so this felt different.

We went there on our first night but it was fully booked, so we booked it for the next night. It was at a slightly later time than what we would usually eat at, but because it had the connotations of being different and niche, we really wanted to visit. This slightly relates to another chapter where I discussed Trip Advisor on restaurants. It hadn't really built up reviews yet which is why we didn't find anything on Trip Advisor, but the fact that it was so different, so niche, is why we ended up there.

We were talking to the owner a little bit and they said that since they've been open they're fully booked 99.9% of the time. They always leave a couple seats for people like us who just turn up, but they were already booked up until the following month. Now I'm pretty sure most of the other hotels didn't have that. Most of the places had open signs. It's surprising that in a saturated market like that, the hotel was offering the same services, but made themselves appear special and niche, to make a huge difference. I think all of us can learn from this. We're probably all in heavily saturated markets now and by doing something slightly different, even if it's just the way we portray ourselves, can make a huge difference to our success.

This leads me into a slightly different example. We have a client who provides a cold calling service, essentially phoning someone who you don't know to try to sell something to them. If we're honest, most of us don't really like those types of people, they're quite pushy and you just want to get them off the phone.

What our client did, which is really different, was niching in, only working with marketing firms or marketing departments. Their service had to be part of a step-by-step process, a long-term goal. They could cold call people to book an appointment, push people onto a website to sign up for a webinar, or to be part of their direct mailing list. The other thing that really makes a difference is that the service is based on a cost per lead. Instead of being paid for a certain day's work, they're being paid on their skill level.

They're stating: "For every person that becomes a qualified lead, you will pay X amount of money to us." All of a sudden, they've removed any of the pain points that their client may have, handling it in a very different way. If you look at their competitors websites, they're all pushing cold calling. They focus on the number of calls they can make in a day, how efficient they can be with what they're doing today, and making sure that people get their maximum number of people called. It's all about the telephone and pushing people. Whereas what our client has done is make the service more about results. They've focused their message on how they link in with current marketing campaigns. They're essentially providing the exact same product, but they're advertising their sales in a different way and since doing so their sales have gone through the roof.

I think this is what's going to become really important. Even if you're not necessarily niching hugely, coming across in a slightly different way to the rest of your market is what's going to be hugely important. I would recommend heading down to Llandudno to check it out and look at the fact that every single place is just a hotel. Try to take on board that we are all in a saturated market that's selling the same thing. The worry will always be 'apples and apples'; the client has nothing to compare to make us anything different. So, how do you guys become the "orange" in the market?

Just to finish off, my one last note is that I always point out to clients that 'customer service' is not a niche. Your argument of 'we provide a better customer service' isn't a niche because nobody goes into business to provide a bad customer service. Therefore, when you say that 'we're different because we really care' or 'we're different because we're providing better customer service than the rest', whilst that may be true, it's not enough for your client.

We need to come up with something that's tangibly different. If customer service is your current niche, I would say that you're marketing isn't strong enough and that you need to think about how you're being portrayed. So good luck and head to Llandudno!

48 HR COMPANIES

This chapter is about changing HR Companies, which we have done recently. When we first set up, we didn't need a HR Company as it was just the directors in business, the two of us. As we started to take on staff, we took on our first HR Company, though probably wrongly looking back. We shopped around for a HR and outsourcing company and went with the cheapest option. What you find with the cheapest option is that you get what you pay for. The issue here is that you'll get a very low service. From our HR Company we received Contracts and a Staff Handbook, copy-and paste style!

This Staff Handbook was probably used for all of their clients, with very few words changed in it. They did the same for our contracts too. We had issues where the contracts they sent for our staff weren't relevant to the jobs they were undertaking; they used a template that they could easily change.

When we first took on the HR Company, we only had one member of staff. Over the years we've had more than fifteen contracts from them and at no point has it occurred to them that we may want a better service or, more importantly, we might be willing to give them more money. I was paying for the HR Company to write contracts, for only around £100 a month, and they provided a helpline for if there were any urgent issues. But because they provided very little to us, never upselling to me or offering me more, I didn't feel comfortable in utilising them or receiving more information from them.

This is one of their biggest issues and I'm sure we all do this; we're used to having a client that might be very small and we forget that companies can grow, which is what every company aims to do. The mistake our HR Company made was that they never acknowledged that we were taking on more staff and potentially required a different service. Over time and after looking around, as soon as someone offered me a better deal, I took it straight away without thinking about it.

We're now paying our new HR Company just over five times what we used to pay and we're receiving a far better service. For our first HR Company, they may have never considered that we were willing to spend this amount of money on HR. Most importantly, we're gaining value from our new HR Company. We're gaining software which allows staff to access and track their holidays, request items and view their bonuses. We're having our contracts correctly re-written and they are also providing three month reviews with our staff to check that everyone is still happy working here.

To learn from this, we may all begin working with a client believing their budget will remain the same over the years. We'll assume that they don't want to spend more money. However, our clients may have grown incredibly, or might have begun to see the value of your service. After seeing results, they may be more willing to invest in you.

We all worry that we can't ask 'The Question' to our client without them looking to move to another supplier. You need to know that this CAN happen, but only if you dramatically raise your costs without reason, causing your client to move elsewhere.

But the difference comes when you increase costs and provide a greater value of service in return. There will always be some form of trigger point. For us, it was having twelve contracts through our HR Company and them still not knowing that we needed a better service. If they had simply upsold me, offering a tailored package that understood our expansion, I would have accepted it. However, as they didn't contact me, I decided to look elsewhere.

This is something we all need to consider. See how this can apply to your business and perhaps try this exercise: Make a list of all of you clients, segment them by how much money they spend on you each year. Then further split up them up according to what services they use. You'll find that perhaps half of your clients don't utilise most of the services you offer. THESE are the clients who can spend more money on your services and, more importantly, the ones who you can provide with more value. Think: Is there something in your service that could dramatically help a client?

RANDOM THOUGHTS

49 BIGGER LOGO

This lesson has been put in to help every design company out there, as I'm sure they all have clients who ask "Can we make the logo larger?" The answer is usually "No!!" and there are plenty of valid reasons for this.

I would actually say that a bigger logo is very much seen as a vanity thing. Clients want to really hammer home that it's them; it's their company and they're comparing themselves to the household businesses in how they portray themselves.

Companies like Nike and Adidas, who are very much all about their brand, are so well know that they don't need to push their products in the same way a smaller company would.

Nike will celebrity-endorse their products. They have celebrities use their products and then slap a big logo on it. That works because we're buying into their brand. We already know what they do, so we just buy further and further into their overall brand.

A small company doesn't have that luxury. A small company isn't world renowned, so they need to instead focus on the benefits that they're providing the customer, explaining the services they offer and who best these services work for. Making the logo larger and taking up lots of space on websites, brochures and other marketing material just means that you're reducing space for the important information!

Try to think of it from your potential customer's point of view; you making the logo larger on your advert or website doesn't give them any indication of what services you provide or how you're better than anyone else. You can therefore see that, although the logo does need to be there, it doesn't need to be the main focus.

Imagine that there are two adverts in a magazine- for simplicity's sake let's say they both sell garden sheds. Company A has a massive logo on their advert and then below that they've fitted a small image of a shed with a phone number and web address, because the logo has taken up so much space. I think you'll agree that this is the usual style of advert that you will see from a company.

The second advert starts with a title explaining that their sheds have a life time guarantee. This is followed by three bullet points listing their benefits, a photo with contact details, and their logo in the bottom right corner (not top left of centre).

If you were a betting man (or woman) which option would you imagine will bring in more leads? Asking for a larger logo is a question every designer must go through and, if I'm honest, it's not the clients' fault. They don't know the logic behind the advert; they just want their company's name out there and so they see the bigger logo as the solution. This logic holds especially true on a website where the logo is in the top left corner. The user knows exactly where it is, so it really doesn't need to take up any more space as they will look at it no matter the size.

I feel this lesson has come across as more of a rant, but here's the golden nugget to finish with: if, instead of having a massive logo to get across your brand, you focus on how you can help these people, the number of leads from your marketing will increase!

Last example I promise: Let's take the business card. The standard layout of these is normally one side dedicated to a logo and the other containing contact details. Why not have your logo slightly smaller and feature the main reason someone should contact you right now? This is far more likely to work than just a logo, even a really, really big logo!

50 5 SECOND RULE

This lesson/chapter is called the five second rule and whether you like to admit it or not, everyone does this in some way or another. So let's explain this first. The idea is that people will make a judgement call on your business within the first five seconds of seeing your website or other marketing mediums. They'll decide if you're credible enough within those five seconds, it's as simple as that. Don't believe me? What's worse is that we all do this when meeting people too; a person doesn't even need to open their mouth and people have already made an assumption about them.

For example, you see a photo of a man and you might either think that he looks nice, or he looks sleazy. You know nothing about him but you've already made that decision. This is sadly a part of life, but guess what? Now that you know this, you can use it to your advantage!

Now, the reasoning behind the five second thoughts needs a little bit of explaining, but the basics are that we make these judgement calls based on our own personal experiences. If you got mugged by someone who looked a certain way, you would be careful of anyone that looked like that from then on. If you were ripped off by a woman who dressed in a certain way and then met another woman who dressed the same, you would understandably not want to work with them. It's just human nature; we're hard wired to protect ourselves.

What's even worse is that we judge people from experiences that we've had from watching films and TV. For example, if I asked you to think of a tough guy or hard man, we'll all probably picture a tall, muscly guy similar in style to 'The Mountain' from Game of Thrones (hopefully you get that reference, if not look him up!) because even if we haven't been in a fight, you know from popular culture that he is expected to look like this.

So the good news is that we can appear more credible, or to have a bigger better business than we actually do because of this. For example, let's image you're an Independent Financial Planner (IFA) and, in theory, you are very good with money. Would you rather work with the guy in the cheap suit who turned up in an old banger of a car or the guy in a brand new tailored suit and a BMW outside? You'd automatically trust the BMW driver more as he portrays what you expect of a quality IFA. The guy in the cheap suit would make you think he doesn't have any money so can't be very good with it.

Now, in the world of the internet, people are even more cut throat. How many of you have looked for a new supplier by typing in what you're after on Google. You'll open the first 10 pages, quickly looking through each one and then close the ones that don't immediately look good, before learning anything about them as a company. When you read that sentence, it probably sounds mad; how can people have any idea of how companies work, or the processes that would run through their heads, based on a few seconds? Well the answer is, they can't, but if you don't look as big or credible as the other guy, then sorry, goodbye!

It's not just about looking great either. The potential customer needs to know if you offer what they're looking for instantly. We have to spell this out to them and that's why you see on a lot of websites nowadays the big title text which sums up their business. For example:

"We're accountants who work exclusively with car garages."

That gives a super clear indication to the user of what you do and who you do it for. Whereas you'll land on a different accounts website and it just has their logo, some pictures of people in suits, and then loads of information on the 20 different services hat they offer. It's all just too messy and will turn users away.

Exercise:

Take a good look at your company and your competitors and look at the people who are smashing it in your industry:

- How do they look?
- How do they dress?
- What does their marketing and website look like?
- Does yours look totally different?
- Are they clearly in a different class to you?
- Or are you stuck in your old ways?

Then now is the time to change. Once you know the best in class and the company that is clearing up, study them and add the best bits into your marketing and appearance.

51 STEAL IDEAS AND RUN WITH THEM!

I tried to come up with a better name for this, but I thought it was best to just be honest with it. If you want to see what your competitors are doing, what they're offering, or how they're communicating with their potential clients, the best and easiest way to do this is to sign up for their email marketing. Any well performing company will know that having a growing database is super important, so join their email list and start learning!

This should be obvious, but please make sure it's not your business email just so that you don't get caught out. Instead, ensure it's a personal email or create a new one.

You'll be surprised at the number of ideas and strategies that they're performing that you've not even thought of. Better yet, they're offering your same services in a different way to how you are. You may notice that actually, their approach and slightly different messaging could work for you. So soak up their ideas and look at how you can improve on them.

It might be that they're categorising by industries and how they help a set industry, whereas you're just offering your services to everyone. It's little, simple ideas like this that makes it worth signing up for.

You're potentially just starting out, or only have a limited budget, so sign up for your competitors' marketing as they'll have already spent money and learnt the lessons that you can take advantage of. It's as simple as that. As business owners, we're always looking at clever and different strategies. In fact, that's why you will have picked this book up.

There's lots of ideas you can run with, but sometimes you really don't need to reinvent the wheel, instead learn from the companies around you and improve upon them.

52 ARE YOU EASY TO PAY?

This question may seem simple, but once you've read this lesson, hopefully you can take a step back and realise that there are still ways that you could make it even simpler for your clients. One of the best things about using a software is that they make it super simple to purchase from them. If you buy some software, let's say 'Slack', they make it really easy for you to pay them. You literally either pay on your card, direct debit, or in a lump sum for some discount.

Now they do offer different levels of service for this amount, but it's super simple and, more importantly, it covers every possible way that someone might want to pay. I think this is the biggest mistake most service companies make. We presume everyone will just pay by BACS. Let me tell you now, if you offer more options and make your pricing transparent, your sales will increase!

Now the argument would be that, unlike a software, a service company is offering a bespoke solution, so that there is no 'one size fits all'. But that doesn't mean we can't provide options for payment. Not only does this make it easier to purchase from you, but it will also mean that clients who previously have not been able to afford you are then an option.

Let's run through the payment options that you should be considering.

1. **The standard one:** Pay a percentage up front, then on completion. This is normally emailed across and then BACS transferred over.

Ways to tweak this:

- Could you change it from two invoices to three to help with cash flow for them?
- Could you take a smaller percentage upfront and more near the end?

2. Allow the user to pay for this as a monthly fee. It works well for yearly services.

Ways to tweak this:

- Have no deposit and just set up a direct debit?
- Could they top up this monthly fee with upsold extras?

3. Have you considered offering a finance package? There is no reason a service company can't offer a finance pack where a potential customer pays over two or three years instead of upfront (just like when purchasing a car or house).

As an example, my company, Strafe Creative, is building a new ecommerce website for a company and its going to cost £50k to build this. We allowed the company to pay this over three years, on a finance agreement instead. The benefit is that our new version of their website will increase sales and, in theory, cover their monthly cost. This means it's a no brainer for them to move forward with the build with us. You can see how making it easier to buy from you can be a win for everyone involved.

Tweaks to this:

- No deposit up front – just a monthly fee
- Charge a premium on this finance option

If you're charging a large amount for a one off service, this is normally a great option.

Can the potential customer pay by card? We think card options are just for retail but lots of companies would either pay quicker, or even spend more, if they could pay on card. The argument would be that you'll have to pay a fee on this, which is true. But the extra money made from allowing the customer to pay there and then in your meeting would be hugely beneficial to most companies.

Allow the user to pay online through your website. Most people think you can only do ecommerce if you have products, but this works really well for a service company too, especially if their prices are fixed. Have some hidden pages on your website which can only be visited if you have the exact link. Then send that link to the customer and they can enter their information and pay. Again, it's just about giving them options!

This lesson is about identifying all of the barriers as to why people don't want to buy from you and fixing those. Most people overlook payment options and just see payment as "if they want my service they will pay". Hopefully, you can start to see how offering these different payment terms link into marketing and sales and therefore how profitable your business will be.

Make life easier for them

If we're going to the trouble of providing these payment options, we want to make them as simple as possible to use as well, so no paper options! Everything should be done online.

For example, we had a client recently where we had to set up a direct debit with them. They sent me a letter with the information, which I then had to fill in and post to them. This meant that I had to pay for postage and also walk to the post box. That's not a huge deal, but it seems madness when you can use a system like 'Gocardless', where you can do the whole thing on a form that you email your client. You can see again how much simpler this is and how likely it is for them to fill in.

Now, this next example is for hairdressers. With most hairdressers, you book in with them and you pay at the end with cash or by card. If it's an expensive haircut, you pay or you go elsewhere, those are the only real options. But what if you could book online and pay for your haircut before you even arrive? I bet that would stop cancellations. What if you offered a direct debit where clients can get a monthly cut and six-monthly dyes for a set monthly price? Again, I bet that would work well for customers For expensive options, like hair extensions, you could do finance options too. These are all ideas that I don't know a single hairdresser offering, but all of these would make life easier for their customers.

Exercise:

What payment options do you currently offer? From the list provided, add in one new option and monitor to see how often people use it. Also, monitor your conversion rate to see if it improves. If it's useful for clients and it's increasing sales, keep it. If not, dump it and try another. You really want at least three months of running with it to know if it's useful or not.

53 THE MATCHSTICK

This lesson is all about giving something purpose and I call this trick 'The Matchstick'. A matchstick has a very set purpose. It's a small piece of wood which you can ignite when you strike it against something and it makes fire. It's made from balsa wood which is super cheap but, because it's been repurposed and used in a slightly different way, companies can charge far more money for it. This is essentially what we're trying to do with our businesses, taking something that we already have and seeing if we can repurpose it to sell for more money.

A really great example is when we worked with a business club that had a thousand members, who made money through their monthly and yearly memberships. They were thinking of ways to get more people involved in buying from them. Previously they had given sponsorship opportunities, where people pay to be promoted by the club through events and pop-up banners. However, they struggled to get people to sign up because it cost thousands of pounds a year to be promoted. The results from this investment weren't very tangible. Instead, they repurposed their sponsorship opportunity through a digital platform, so that the club's email marketing campaigns were 'sponsored by X'. This included the sponsor's logo and link to their site. It made the investment trackable and brought their sponsor's message to a targeted market. As it was repurposed, the club could charge a lot more money for it.

This links back to the matchstick. Suddenly, it's not just a standard piece of wood, you can make fire from it. Instead of charging a few pence you can charge a pound for it.

Another unusual example of this is a client of ours who owned a cardboard box company. They sold both standard and elaborate cardboard boxes to packaging companies. Over the years, work became much quieter. Competitors from other countries offered cheaper product and transport costs. To tackle this, they gave their cardboard a different purpose. They started making cardboard celebrity masks on the side for some extra money. They used good quality cardboard and string, rather than cheaper material, and sold them to fancy dress shops for around £4 a pack, which is absolutely outrageous. This idea exploded and the markup value caused them to make millions. They've since sold the company, essentially a small factory which sells cardboard, for around £5 million. By repurposing their product and service, it changed their business massively.

It relates to one of the other chapters where we spoke about niching in. It's about looking at every little part of your business and how it can be repurposed for something more profitable.

So what's the matchstick in your business? What are you or your clients currently underappreciating that should really be its own, awesome standalone service?

54 THE KIT KAT

Now before I go into this, I have to hold my hands up and say that I've fallen for the Travelodge premium option far too many times and they always get me! I think it's because I love how simple it is.

For anyone who isn't in the UK (or potentially do live in the UK but live under a rock) Travelodge essentially have the business hotel market to themselves. They position their hotels on motorways or in locations where business people will need them. They're of a good quality but aren't over-the-top. Plus they serve a good full English breakfast! Their beds are comfy and I use them a lot when I'm traveling around.

Re-reading this it reads like I'm a brand ambassador, sorry about that! But this is the bit that gets me every time. They offer a premium room and do you know what makes those rooms premium? Well, not much to be honest!

They give you slightly faster free wifi, they sometimes have slightly different bedding, some different shampoos and a KitKat. That's right, you read it here first, a bloody Kit Kat! That's what they consider premium?!

You know what, if I'm given the option, I normally take it, as that different bedding is super comfy, the shampoos are better, I use the wifi anyway so it may as well be faster, and who doesn't absolutely love a Kit Kat?!

The cost for them to do this? Nothing, at the most a few quid. They already have the wifi in, they're just scaling it back for the other rooms, so there's no real cost there. I doubt the different linen is much more and I wouldn't be surprised if the shampoo was the same as the standard room but in a nicer bottle. Of course there is the Kit Kat too, so I'm going to be overly kind and say they spend £4 per room extra (I bet it's more like 4p as they do it on such a huge scale). You know what that costs me as the end user? An extra £20 per night! The cost is small enough for me to not worry and they make a huge profit margin on me from it.

Looking at our own service-based companies, what is your businesses Kit Kat?

What I love about this is that they've really drilled down to what people want when they arrive. They want a soft bed, a nice shower, and something sweet to eat as they're tired from travelling. So let's simplify your business down to the basics shall we?

Interior designers, your clients want little to no involvement. They want it to last. They're probably house proud and most importantly they want to impress. They will want people to know that they hired an interior designer. Knowing this, why don't you, as you're going along, take photos of the room taking shape and have a small photobook produced, showing the transformation. The cost to you is around £20 for the book. It will take 30 minutes to use an online printer to produce the book . You can charge them £250 and call it 'Your journey book', which they can keep on their coffee table to impress their friends who come round. It's a win for them, a small extra cost in relation to what they've already spent, and of course the profit margin is huge on it too.

Exercise:

- For your main service, why do people use your service? Be honest here, what are the real reasons if you're really honest?
- Now that you've got them down on paper, what could you offer them to further enhance those reasons? When we try to provide additional items or services to enhance those key reasons, they picked the original service, so that's where we can see big profits!
- Give it a go and find your Kit Kat.

P.s. Send me Kit Kats and I'll love you for life!

55 RESTAURANT IN LONDON

This lesson doesn't necessarily fall into a chapter, consider it a bonus one. I went to London recently to see Aladdin as a birthday present from my wife. Afterwards, we were looking for somewhere to eat and I began to realise how the restaurant industry markets itself very differently to perhaps just five years ago.

Back then we might have arrived in a new city, walked around, chosen a restaurant that didn't look too busy and got a seat. This is a thing of the past now. Instead, we arrived in London and wandered around a bit, but I had my phone out, looking up every restaurant we saw online to see their reviews. We eventually went to a coffee shop just to look on Trip Advisor, filtering down our location, prices and types of food. This really interesting paradigm shift shows that a business' whole appearance and how it is portrayed is more important nowadays. People are willing to completely believe the judgment of a stranger through their reviews and recommendations. We now live in a world where we are far more likely to go with a stranger's recommendation than try something for ourselves.

Whilst this is slightly worrying, it is also really exciting. It means that us business owners can begin planning how to look as credible as possible. We can make sure that everyone, not just restaurants, has reviews in place. Clients may no longer just want a meeting with you. They may also require some form of online reviews to assess your company first.

On our next day, we had a wander to find a brunch-style place to eat, something that London isn't short of. We decided not to use Trip Advisor this time, keeping our phones in our pockets, and walked around instead. We suddenly experienced a very different way of purchasing something. We stopped looking at the menus and based our decision on how a place looked. We looked at whether a restaurant had invested in quality signs and whether their exterior looked nice, as it suggested that they had put more money and time into their food as well.

This is potentially the wrong way to think about it but the old saying of 'don't judge a book by its cover' is actually very true. We are more likely to come to an assumption on how good a quality something is, based on its appearance. Even with the first way we researched restaurants, we only used Trip Advisor for restaurants that already looked appealing to us. If somewhere didn't look nice, they had already lost a customer by not making an effort. I know this beautiful restaurant in Covent Garden, which had foliage and a lovely canopy outside. It looked very quaint and you could tell a little bit of effort had been put in. These extra features were all it took for us to go inside, as it appeared to stand out from the other, more standard, places. When you go to London you probably do want something a little bit more special. I think we all underestimate how important appearance is, not just for our standard marketing or for web. When someone meets you for the first time, they'll make split-second decisions based on if you're credible and knowledgeable, deciding if they want to work with you.

As you can see, this all links into the idea that human perception is so important and that we only have a couple of seconds for someone to make a decision on if they want to work with us or not.

Picking a restaurant can be related to choosing any service. As much research as we do, we also base our decision on how something looks. I recommend thinking about how you select a restaurant. Do you go off a recommendation or do you use your friends' suggestions? Would you look on Facebook, social media, or Trip Advisor to see reviews? Or would you just turn up on the day and have a look around. It's likely that whatever you're doing, other people will be doing as well. You can take some of these learnings and apply them to your own business. If you don't have online reviews, generate some. Consider how the outside of your shop or the outside of your office looks like as people's perceptions of you are really important. We live in a world where we have to buy nice things or own expensive items to be perceived in a certain way. For example, even when Strafe Creative was first set up, I always made sure I had a nice car, as clients would want to see that we were successful. I felt that this was a way of appearing more credible and it made me feel more confident. Clients bought our services more when we turned up to meetings in nice cars. I take this as a marketing budget rather than worrying that it is a big expenditure. As long as you know why you're spending that money, the investment can be a success.

So have a think about this lesson. Perhaps write down how you could improve your appearance and the reasons for investing money into it.

56 BOOKING.COM
SOCIAL PROOFING

This one is a short lesson, ripped straight from booking.com. It's a place where you can book hotel rooms and apartments. However, it has some really clever features that I think we could all learn from.

Firstly, it tells you how many people have booked a place in the last hour, allowing you to see the really popular places. This builds a company's social proofing, which we've already touched upon, and puts you at ease because you know people are already booking there so it must be ok.

Now, this idea is obviously not going to be so easy for us to do with our much smaller businesses. However, we can definitely still utilise this. For example, we could have an online counter that updates the number of monthly clients we have. Or the counter could also update the number of websites we have online, or the amount of money we keep saving clients.

So this quick little lesson makes us think about how we can use numbers in the buying window, especially on our websites. It'll be one of the first things a person sees and it's a great way to build your credibility through social proofing.

57 THE BOOKMARK TRICK

Anytime you come across a clever advertisement or website by someone who's offering you something slightly different, you make the effort of bookmarking it in your browser. I go quite far with mine: I will bookmark something and place it under certain categories. For example, I'll have bookmarks for an idea that I think would work well for a certain industry or for certain types of companies. This method works well because I can use the ideas I've found to send to my clients, or potential clients. This is nice as it shows that you really care and that something has reminded you of them. Sometimes, I will bookmark an idea to wait for the right moment to share it with a client.

I'll always have these ideas to pass back to clients, showing I care about what I do. It links to the rule that it takes seven-nine touch points for someone to buy from you. You have to constantly engage with them, sharing valuable content to hopefully make them want to work with you. Now this idea works well for me because I'm in the marketing and design industry, but you can apply this to most sectors. For example, if you're a property investor then you might find information about certain types of houses or tax benefits that you can send across to a client.

It's important to provide as much value and help as possible without selling to them. If you're at the front of their mind then they will feel inclined to help you out in return. This links to a famous term coined by BNI called 'Givers Gain'. It refers to giving value that helps people and having the help returned to you. This idea is also quite famous from the book 'The Secret' by Ronda Byrne, which is definitely worth reading. She explains that if you're always helping people, the world will always find a way to help you back. I constantly bookmark anything that might be helpful and then once every two weeks sit down to look through them, working out who these ideas could work for. Some of the bookmarked ideas won't be perfect for a client there and then, so you can hold on to them until the right moment. Others will be perfect to send out to people and can cause a discussion that might lead to a project with which you can help them. You can see how quickly doing something as simple as this can help build up more discussions and more work for you all - so good luck!

58 FREE COFFEE

In this chapter, we're going to discuss 'value added', again talking about one of my favorite things: Food!

We buy breakfast for our staff and there are a range of different places for us to choose from, especially in Nottingham City Centre. Wherever you go, you'll receive the same things: bacon or sausage sandwiches (cobs if you're from the Midlands!), porridge or a fruit salad. What's most important is the places that we end up buying from.

There is a slight caveat to this. We work with a coffee company who told us that to make a cup of coffee costs around 10p. This covers the cup, coffee, milk, and hot water. Because of how demanding this market is, certain companies would make a lot of money by selling this for several pounds, though I'm not suggesting that you change from this strategy if you do this. I've discovered that some clever cafes are instead pricing their sandwiches slightly higher, again for several pounds, but including a 'free' coffee with it. It's this value-added that makes it feel like you're receiving a lot for your money. If you visited somewhere else and bought a coffee separately you may end up paying only 70p more, but we go back to the companies that provide us with more value for money.

Starbucks and similar cafes don't necessarily sell their coffee, they sell the experience of sitting down and being in a nice environment. But if you're a place which focuses on selling your food and drink, you'll encourage more people to visit by creating items with value-added.

We can take lessons from this with our internal processes. For example; with running Strafe Creative, a design agency, instead of giving clients discounts (which I never recommend you offering) we can provide value-added services. We could include hosting for a year to help save our clients some money, or offer some extra software such as live-chat. This doesn't cost us anything because we've already built it, but we would normally charge a little bit for this.

There are lots of services like this that you can add into your own business that you've already spent time creating. By providing clients with added value, you can appear different in the market whilst making your clients feel like they are getting more for their money. So, see how value-added can help your company.

59 SUPERMARKETS

More food related lessons - sorry people! I'll discuss the process of buying food and the lessons I've learnt along the way that can apply to your business.

Whilst recently in Italy, I visited a supermarket and found that it was a very different buying experience to what we have in the UK. UK supermarkets revolve around convenience; everything's prepared for you. For example, when buying carrots, you'll buy ones already cut up, cleaned, ready to use or frozen. The Italian way is very different: The focus is on fresh produce. The carrots may not be cleaned, they may still have their leaves on, and they aren't pre-packaged. They come in beautiful wooden crates that have clearly just come from the farm. You weigh them on a scale, put a sticker on them, then the rest is done at the till. This experience is far more organic and pleasant, making the food feel better quality. The UK media dislikes anything that doesn't look perfect, but in Italy they accept differently shaped and sized food. I'm sure the reason the food tastes better is because of the placebo effect of how I had to purchase it.

The reason I emphasise this experience is because of how it relates to our businesses. We presume the focus is mainly on our products and the services we provide. If you're an accountant, we believe completing the books on time is enough. We're a website agency and we used to feel that as long as we built a website, theoretically the project was a success. But actually, we should focus more on the client-buying experience. We should focus on the experience that the users/customers get taken through, by you, to purchase and beyond.

There are so many parts that need to be to be taken into account that make a huge difference.

For example, we've worked hard on making our feedback process incredibly simple for our clients. As you can imagine, the feedback process for a design project used to be quite difficult for us. Feedback had to be provided in person, on the phone, or potentially over email – all of which could easily get lost in translation. We now use software in which the client can click directly onto the designs, pinpointing exactly where their feedback relates to, and write their comment. We can reply, agreeing with the request or recommending other options. By identifying problems in your current level of service and tweaking the process, you will create a much nicer experience for your customer. This is what Italian supermarkets do really well. Having a smooth and pleasant process, helped by trained people, ensures a slightly different, and definitely better, experience.

To apply this to your business, write down your full customer journey. From when you first meet a client to the sales process, and through to when they begin working with you. What touch points do they get? Do you welcome them into the project with anything? Also, consider how often you get in touch with them and what happens at each stage of the process. What happens if they are a recurring customer compared to if they no longer work with you? All of these elements need to tie in with each other to create a consistent business flow. Then you can begin to understand how to improve in certain areas: You'll be amazed at how many steps you've missed. For example, you may be happy that you have a new client on board, but then you haven't actually done anything to onboard them. You haven't sent them anything to say thanks and you haven't given them an idea of the process. There are lots of small issues like this that can build up, to influence how likely someone is to buy from you again. So, write out your full process then identify the areas that you could potentially improve on. I don't recommend improving everything in one go; instead pick one small area to improve on, whether that's introducing a piece of software, creating a new process, or sending a certain email at a certain time. Once you've improved on one area, move on to fixing the next issue. So, give it a go!

60 WAITING LISTS

This last idea is a very popular one that's used in software companies: waiting lists. Here's the reason why SAAS companies originally did this. When testing software, there would be an alpha testing stage where a very small number of people would try out software and give feedback on how to improve it. When companies got to a stage where they need more people to test it, but couldn't fully release it to the public, they did Beta testing. People would sign up to try out the software, but because companies only wanted a certain number of people on the system at one time, they would have to create a waiting list. Naturally, people wanted to sign up for this waiting list because they wanted to feel first in line for getting hold of something that other people can't have. There's a sense of premium, that something must be good if you have to wait for it.

It's important to advertise the delay for a product or service as a waiting list. Instead of apologising for the delay, you can explain that there is a waiting list for your service because you're so popular. It's that shift in how you explain this to a potential client that makes you feel really premium, making more people sign up to you.

For small businesses that are reading this, there will be stages when you are really busy and stages when you aren't. When you're busy you don't want to push people away by just apologising for the delay. A waiting list can make this delay a selling point. Instead of ignoring the issue by telling a client you can get the job done and letting them down, make them aware of the waiting list. Nine times out of ten, once they know the reasoning's, clients are fine with the wait because it makes your service feel premium.

A good example of this comes from one of our clients. They are a property developers, but also do some investment work. They decided to put a lot of their money into building properties and then selling them to make more money, making good mark-ups on them. They made the decision to use other people's money to help with this, so that they weren't financially burdened by the investments and so that they could grow quicker. As soon as they mentioned this idea to others, lots of people wanted to join, and our client said yes to them all. The problem with this is that their team could only do a certain number of projects every couple of months. Then people were becoming annoyed that they'd given our client a lot of money, but weren't seeing the returns as quickly as they wanted to.

After working out an average of how many projects they could take on a year, our client made themselves appear exclusive. People would now have to pay to join their waiting list, costing 10% of the overall project. Our client said it was one of the best things they ever did because they appeared more premium and their waiting lists grew and grew. To put people off joining, the fee to join the waiting list increased to 50% upfront, even though their project wouldn't start for six months. However, the waiting list didn't slow down and it continued to be very successful. At the time of writing this, our client now takes 100% off people, who are on a waiting list for a year and a half, before their project begins and they see any return.

Of course, the people investing from £50,000-£100,000 in our client are wealthy people and are looking at the long term. But it just shows how well waiting lists can work and how you can use them to your advantage to appear at the top of your game.

My company, Strafe Creative, does something very similar. Instead of apologising that we're busy at the moment, we explain that on certain projects there's a small waiting list. Clients will be added to the waiting list if they wish to move forwards. We explain the average waiting time to them, which is no more than two months. For a design agency, instead of steering away from the issue and taking on the project, we steer into the issue. We believe that it's a good thing that people need to wait because it means we're popular and that people want to work with us. It allows us to take our time on the projects that we want to do. I think that's an excellent lesson that anyone can take from this.

There will be lots of ways that you can apply this to your business. Have a think about how you could potentially make use of a waiting list at your company; though it depends on what stage you are currently at. When you have little work, you can use other lessons from this book, but as you get busier and busier, this lesson is a great idea to keep momentum without annoying any potential clients.

FINAL THOUGHTS

61 KEEP GOING!

A weird way to end this book but you are going to fail with some of these hacks. Some will fail due to how they were implemented whilst others just won't suit your company. But keep pushing through, keeping experimenting, and don't be afraid to fail.

It's hard to put into words, but the book you're reading has taken 14 months to write. I wrote the book in fits and starts. I'd work on it solidly for a month then not touch it for another month or two. I would make excuses not to do it with the worry of failure, or I would have an idea for a chapter but couldn't think of the best way to get across my message. I'd get stuck on the chapter which in turn ruined my confidence for a bit. The best way to overcome this? Just keep pushing through. Life loves a fighter and you have to be willing to do the things that others won't do.

A great example of this is cold calling. You could have 20 calls to make and the first 19 are all flat no's. It would be easy to give up and say that cold calling doesn't work for your business. But actually, on that 20th call you get a yes, go to meet them, and get a big project from it. We all need those no's so we can learn from them. If anything, those previous 19 calls were the training you needed to be able to make that 20th call perfect.

This book is full of ideas and I know if you stick with them they'll deliver for you. But you've got to be willing to test and experiment with them. Let's take an advert for example. You're an accountant and you run an advert with an image of someone working from a laptop, along with the message 'work with us'. It gets no responses, so you run it again with a photo of your team instead. It still doesn't work, so you run it again with an image of your logo. Again, it doesn't work so you run it with some photos of money and all of a sudden you're getting leads!

Most people aren't willing to experiment. They'll try something once and if it fails, they chalk it up to "Not working for their industry" and move onto another idea. But stick with it and be willing to fail as you'll be surprised at your results.

Guess what though? You're here reading this book right now, you've got to the end of it, and hopefully you've been trying out some of the ideas as you've been going, so now what?

Well get putting these into action. Do only one at a time and test it until you know if it works for you or not. Working at one at a time will ensure each idea gets the attention it deserves. Find one that works? Throw money and resources at it and see how much you can squeeze out of it. Once you've got it performing amazingly get someone else to run it. Then move onto creating another marketing pillar for your business with another of these chapters. Eventually you'll have multiple avenues of leads and you'll be able to turn these off and on like a tap! Now that's the perfect business!

I also want to personally thank you for taking the time to purchase and read my book. To me, this has been the most personal thing I've ever done. I've put myself out there and it's taken over a year of my life to do.

I want to hear from you guys so get in touch on Instagram at rossalexdavies and I'll get back to you as quickly as I can. I'd love to hear your thoughts and questions so hopefully I'll hear from you guys soon.

Good luck with your business and remember to keep pushing forward!

ABOUT THE AUTHOR

Ross Davies was shortlisted for the Amazon Young Entrepreneur Award in 2016. He's winner of the 2016 Abundance award and the Midlands Creative Business of the Year award, as well as being listed as one of the 100 Rising Stars. He is a design agency owner, a partner at a second marketing firm, a lecturer at Nottingham Trent University, a council member in Nottingham UK and an expert paper plane maker.

Stop looking for more to read and go
action some of these ideas!

Made in the USA
Middletown, DE
06 September 2018